ARRIVAL PRESS

YORKSHIRE

Edited

By

TRUDI RAMM

First published in Great Britain in 1994 by
ARRIVAL PRESS
1 - 2 Wainman Road, Woodston,
Peterborough, PE2 7BU

All Rights Reserved

Copyright Contributors 1994

Foreword

Poetry in Motion - Yorkshire is a collection of poems that gives the reader an insight into how the *locals* feel about the area that they live in. Among the poems about the landscape nestle works about the people; their lifestyle and their feelings towards living where they do.
By reading the poems included in this anthology I was given a vivid mental picture of what each area looked like and how it would feel to be there. A couple of the poems made me want to catch the next train!

I am sure that you will enjoy reading *Poetry in Motion - Yorkshire* and that each time you dip into its pages you will find a new delight to fuel your imagination. Reading this book is like taking a trip to Yorkshire in the comfort of your armchair!

Trudi Ramm
Editor

CONTENTS

Title	Author	Page
Yorkshire Trough And Through	Janet Spears	1
Yorkshire	Elaine Jane Potter	2
Ode To Flo And Stan	Ann Greaves	3
The West Riding	Edward Littlewood	4
The Pennine M62	R W Eaves	4
Spring Comes To Yorkshire	Patricia Mary Clark	5
West Yorkshire	Ivy Singer	6
Aunts On Parade - Or A Yorkshire Wedding	Janette Meek	6
Odd Shaped Hills	Barbara Grice	7
What Yorkshire Means To Me	Irene Taylor	8
Lee Gap Fair	Peggy Hunter	9
Yorkshire Moors	Jean Venables	10
A Miner's Advice To His Son	Fred Lunn	10
A Southerner's Point Of View	Evelyn Tranter	11
Circa York	Jean Heaven	12
Swan Song	Charles Maries	13
Our Yorkshire Bits	E Bell	14
Yorkshire Moors	Agnes Solan	15
Exile	Eileen Walters	16
Unsighted	T E Armitage	17
I The Humber Bridge	V Aston	18
My Town	Phyllis Mosley	19
The Buttress Blues	W H Metcalfe	20
Yorkshire Bred	Ryan Bartram	21
Nigel's Ghost	James C Goff	22
Winter Bleak In Heptonstall	Stuart Marriott	23
Market Day	Dawn England	24
Filey	Lorraine Robertshaw	25
Dalby Forest	Mary L Burton	26
West Yorkshire	Mary Reynolds	27
The Mill	Margaret Hooper	28
Scouting For Mothers	Hilary Shields	29

Me Dad	Jean M Senior	30
A Walk In Yorkshire	Judith M Rudge	31
Untitled	Shirley Harrison	32
My Pennine Roots	Catherine Howard	33
The Silent Looms	Joyce Hefti Whitney	34
A Dream Fulfilled	Anne Isobel Dawson	35
The Place For Me	Elizabeth Ryan	36
Yorkshire Year	John Keeble	37
Cathedral Graves	Kate Ibbeson	38
A Favourite Place	Jean Leathley	39
The Minster: York	Joyce Atkinson	40
Join Us For A Beer	Dorothy Shaw	41
Tankersley	W Ullyott	42
Our Castle	Benny Wilkinson	43
A Bit Abah't Barnsley	Roy Portman	44
Forget The Dales	Keith Stokes	45
Tale Of A Yorkshire Hubby	Annie Storey	46
A Tear For The Miners	James Cann	47
Recollections of Bately (West Yorks)	Rosamond Cox	48
Yorkshire	Muriel Jenkins	49
From New To Old	Arnold Price	50
Old Tom	Karl Hague	51
Throstles Nest (Another Name For Bingley)	Winston White	52
Beautiful Yorkshire	June Alethea Nichols	53
Wakefield Town	Ellen Hinnighan	54
The Minor Pleasures of Hull	J Pietrusiak	55
A Tribute To York	Patricia Surman	56
A View Of The Dales	Edward Ramsey	57
It's A Wonderful Place . . .	Ann Johnson	58
Bingley	Mary Jackson	59
Brotherton	Butch	60
Edge Of The Moors	Florence Needler	61
Nostalgic Memories (Gran's)	M M Walker	62
Bingley Upon Aire	R Whitehead	63
Untitled	A Mitchell	64

Title	Author	Page
Football Supporter	Audrey Gamble	65
Doncaster Market	June Tomlinson	66
Ryedale	Eva Ward	67
The Return	Ronald Gatenby	68
Inheritance	Denise Stables	69
Sleeping Pavements	L B Vickers	70
Belated Protest	Alan Holdsworth	71
Semer Water	John Avison	72
Lines Written In A Country Village	Rod Cooper	73
Yorky's Lament	Colin Moore	74
A Thought For Yorkshire	Janet Davison	75
The Rentman	Allen Tortice	76
Destination	Theresa Sowerby	76
From The East To The North	Catherine Mitchell	77
Landscape In A Quarry	Pauline Fletcher	78
My Yorkshire	Colin Garner	79
Norther Yorkshire	Mary H Wood	79
Family Outing	Ruth P Singer	80
The Ghost Of Acaster Airfield	Genevieve Grewer	80
York Minster	Joan Clark	81
The Countryside	Mark Evans	82
Yorkshire	Sheila Stead	82
Westerly heritage	F Sexton	83
The Yorkshire Show	John David Bone	83
Hill Spell	Neville Slack	84
Roche Abbey	C G Crehan	84
Wuthering Heights	Dorothy Nixon	85
Yorkshire	Elsa Rhodes	85
Denholme - A Yorkshire Village	Kate Heaton	86
Changes At Heptonstall	John Brandon	86
Yorkshire Spirit	Stuart J Firth	88
Yorkshire Snippets	Molly Smithson	88
Me Roots	Josie Brown	89
Untitled	Audrey Loxton	89

West Yorkshire Muck	Gail Mary Leadley	90
Where There's Muck	J Addison	90
Yorkshire	Maureen Beaumont	91
Home Of Mine	Barbara Ward	91
The Whinmoor Way	Mark Allinson	92
Spirit Of Life	Jarusi Warburton	92
This Yorkshire Moor	Mandy Huggins	93
Yorkshire Way	Mary Powell	94
Approaching Helmsley - Evening	Elizabeth Lester	94
Thoughts Of Yorkshire	Angela Melvin	95
End Of An Era	Ian Mylchreest	95
Sonnet To Spring	E M Fearnley	96
Night In A Northern Town	Tracy Atkinson	96
Home (Laisterdyke)	Jean Dunbar	97
The Valesman	Richard Lung	98
The Ex-Pat	Mick Freeman	98
Untitled	K Hudson	99
Ribblehead Viaduct	Philip Dacre	99
Our Yorkshire Heritage	Phoebe Roberts	100
South Yorkshire	Winifred Heeley	101
Sheffield - Now And Then	Doreen Wright	102
York	John Rayne-Davis	103
Yorkshire x 4	Angela Feather	104
The Last Shift	Monique C Richardson	104
Scarborough	Robert Messruther	105
The Valley	Bess Beecroft	106
Jackdaws Round St Leonard's Spire	Mary Newton	106
Yorkshire	Joy Duggleby	107
Malham	M Platts	108
The Ridings	Ursula M Badger	108
Scarborough Castle	Jess Chambers	109
Images In Stone	Barbara France	109
From A Yorkshire Tyke	Samuel Fullwood	110
Spring Song	Mary Found	110
Happy In Hebden	Bryan Green	111
North Yorkshire Morning	D Hair	112

Title	Author	Page
Hebden Bridge	Fay Fielding	112
The Miner	Charles Roshy	113
See	Margaret Northern	113
A Country Lane In Autumn	Margaret Gott	114
Nature's Trail	Pam Reynolds	114
Huddersfield My Town	Lily Mansfield	115
Dreaming	Emma Ward	116
A Treasured Life	Hilary Wood	116
Untitled	D Beardsley	117
The Chocolate Bar	Marion Warke	118
Free Today	Hilda Mary Regan	118
A Song	Lynda Billard	119
Sheffield	Claire Robinson	120
Bygone Trains	Roy Blackman	120
The Yorkshire That I Love	Thomas Wells	121
Leisure Treasure	V Clarke-Irons	122
Scarborough	Jeremy Ward	122
Filey Bay	Glenda Lawrence	123
Home County	Doreen Wilson	124
Ode To A Northern Town	Helen Burke	124
Memories	Marion Elliott	125
Barnsley	Patrick Sykes	126
Our Earth	Cecil Wadsworth	127
A Yorkshire Poem	Walter Smith	128
Times On The Hambleton Hills 1940-1944	Gwenda L Mather	129
Houghton Woods (East Riding Of Yorkshire)	Jean Blackburn	130
Yorkshire	S C Riley	130
Bygone Bradford	B McGough	131
Yorkshire	Lynette Griffiths	131
Untitled	Florence Watson	132
North Riding Resurrection	Daphne Parker	132
Move Over, Wordsworth!	Bill Stanton	133
Our Town	Knighton Joyce	134
Spring Storm	Bez Hinnighan	135
A Beautiful Place	Clare Barnett	136
Temple Newsam - Leeds	Audrey Organ	136

Title	Author	Page
Requiem	Mary Wood	137
Bempton	Marjorie Corrie	138
York Minster	Sean de Podesta	138
Fish	Delia Rutlidge	139
Cursed Into Bastardy	Iris E Limb	140
Our Environment	A G Ede	140
The City Of Leeds	M Mason	141
Untitled	M Staddon	142
A Taste Of Yorkshire	Julia A Smith	142
Bygone - By'eck	Andrew J Massey	143
Me 'N' Yorkshire	Maureen Smith	144
Black Hill	Christine Ross	144
Silence Of The Trams	Anne Sharman	145
Bridlington	Irene Patricia Kelly	146
Yorkshire Yearning	P J Krumins	147
Lines About A Line	Mldred Holmes	147
North Yorkshire	Ruth Margaret Rhodes	148
The Mill	Ron Lister	148
Andy Capp Pub Patter	Dorrie McMenemy	149
What Yorkshire Means To Me	Jean Russell	150
Hebden Bridge	Angela Sutcliffe	150
My Yorkshire	Joan Machen	151
Desolation	Raymond Softley	152
Surrounding Huddersfield	Joan M Middleton	152
Rain Over The Yorkshire Moors	Stephen Dyson Taylor	153
Robinwood	Janice Bailey	154
Yorkshire (We Are Two Of A Kind)	James Lee	154
A Celebration Of North Yorkshire	Angela McLaughlin	155
Valentine To Scarborough	Ted Harben	156
Moorland Sheep	J T Gatenby	157
Pit Fire	Mary Froggett	157
The Yorkshire Scene	Kathleen Rudd	158
The Yorkshire Seasons	Dennis dunham	158
Wat	Catherine A Lovett	159

Yorkshire	Winifred V Hipwell	160
The Yorkshire Pud	Marjorie Langhorn	160
A Memory Of The Dales	Caroline Suzanne Collins	161
The Haworth Spirit	Montague M Richards	162
Just Another Town	C Whitaker	162
Wet Sunday Evening In Thirsk	Elizabeth Haines	163
Chat With A Pheasant	Beryl Clayton	164
Barnoldswick Via Colne	Albert Thornton	165
Barlby In December	Elizabeth Ryan	166
Mother Rother Smother	Terence David Marshall	167
Working Class Heroes	P G Smith	167
Home	Christine Yeoman	168
Dales Inn Tale	Margaret Foreman	169
We're All Bitter	Deborah Scott	170
A Journey Up Wharfedale	Susan Collen-Mawer	170
Rotherham Memories	Anne Crehan	171
Hebden Bridge 1994	Margaret Walker	172
Yorkshire	Mary Thompson	173
Life In South Yorkshire	Keith Frederick Stringer	174
A Special Skill	Edna Beach	175
Halfway House Twixt North And South	Cynthia Cooksley	176
Willowherb	John Browne	177

YORKSHIRE THROUGH AND THROUGH

It's plain to see I'm a Yorkshire lass
brought up on stodge and stout
my broad accent proclaims my class
of where I'm from there's no doubt

Sheffield . . . my place of birth
reared among the grime and smog
I suffer no fools . . I give them wide berth
to any just cause I'll give some clog

Blunt, open, always to the point
a gift from a parent dear
no silver spoon did me anoint
my life was clear cut . . . . of work I'd no fear

The slums were my playground
for many it was their home
those back to back dwellings all around
the seeds of poverty firmly sown

I'm down to earth, no airs and graces
I can look anyone in the eye
proud of my roots . . no matter the places
resolute, steadfast, straight as a dye

The steelworks of Attercliffe were my daily forage
it was the bread and butter of Yorkshire folk
my mother a *grinder* she had such courage
the exhaustion she endured was beyond a joke

My mother's struggle to exist gave me a grounding
to instil in me that Yorkshire grit
giving me the guts to withstand life's poundings
I battled my way through, to no defeat did I submit.

Janet Spears

YORKSHIRE

What does living in North Yorkshire mean to me?
Well, now then, let's see,
I come from Acomb, a village near York
Tourists say how funny I do talk,
But I am proud of my Yorkshire twang
I come from an elite gang,
Last of the Summer Wine, Emmerdale and Heartbeat
All filmed in Yorkshire for the viewers such a treat,
To see the beautiful dales, magnificent countryside
People world-wide now in Yorkshire do reside,
Emily Bronte was inspired up on the moors
See their home with one of our tours,
Wuthering Heights a classic of a book
And all because of the moors, so go take a look,
Roast beef and Yorkshire pud
It looks good and by golly it does yer good,
Sink yer teeth into our grub, wash it down with our ale
Listen to our old folk, they won't half tell you a tale,
Of Yorkshire old and new, young and old
Such stories you will be told,
A day in Yorkshire, there's so much you can do
Take it slowly or take it fast it's up to you,
York Minster, *The Shambles* or *The Bar Walls*
You will know when a visit to York calls,
York isn't going anywhere, it's staying here for you to see
Such magnificent city surrounded by history,
So come to see the white rose city
If you don't it will be such a pity,
Your loss is our gain
So please visit us again and again . . .

Elaine Jane Potter

ODE TO FLO AND STAN

They came from different counties,
Yet met in neither one.
The Yorkshire Rose encompassed them,
'Twas there it all begun.

They settled first at Odsal Top
In t' days when it were noted
for being Wembley o' the north,
streets lined wi' fans devoted.

Then news at new estate were telled,
In Buttershaw, up yonder;
They med their minds up straight away,
No need to stop and ponder . . .

'Cos three-bedroomed home were offered,
Wi' a lovely country view;
A thro' lounge down at bottom,
Upstairs - an inside loo!

In troubled times they struggled thro;
They lived from day to day:
But, needn't worry any more.
For we all turned out OK.

So, this is by way of *thank you*
for all your time and care;
You made it possible for us
To prosper, strive and share . . .

Six ways in all of our troubles,
Six ways in all of our glee;
So, six times, however many,
Say, *well done* - we're glad were me.

Ann Greaves

THE WEST RIDING

From the high, windy moors
On a cold, November night
To the centre of the city
Where the lights are shining bright
From the motorways and highways
Where the cars go flashing by
To the back street of the old town
Where grey poverty is nigh
From the discos and night-clubs
With the young and happy people
To the old and sombre church clock
In its great majestic steeple
There is every sort of person
That you could wish to find
With accents from the Oxford
To the real old Yorkshire kind
The greetings may be genteel
With a soft manicured hand
Or it could be, 'How's tha going lad?
Tha's looking proper grand.'
The ways of life are varied
In these broad and ancient acres
From the whiz-kids with computers
To the old, wooden clog makers.

Edward Littlewood

THE PENNINE M62

The long haul up the hill, in the early morning light,
Gives me quite a thrill as the red rose turns to white.
Ripponden is signed from Junction 22,
And shortly I'll find Yorkshire's finest view.

The tangerine snake with moving silver scales,
Fades as dawn breaks, to a grey shade of pale.
Cruising downhill, piling on the speed,
Moss Moor is passed, the sheep try to feed.

Who'd live on that farm, amidst the motorway?
A lonely house of charm, at least it is fine today.
Over Scammonen Dam, the wind it fairly blows,
Rocking every van, causing them to slow.

Yachts and their slaves turn circles in the well,
The reservoir waves all travellers farewell.
Climb and climb and climb toward the final brow,
Engines hum a rhyme, the heather takes a bow.

Outlane rears its head, showing off some horses,
Executives love to tread on the local courses.
Quiet Huddersfield is left behind Fixby Woods,
Loads and loads of weft are moved by heavy goods.

Then Rastrick trickles down and ends up in the Calder,
Joined to Brighouse town, my home fire starts to smoulder.
Junction 25 at last! I can see my journey's end.
The corn unloads quite fast. Sleep, sweet dreams descend.

R W Eaves

SPRING COMES TO YORKSHIRE

Draw the curtain and there it is,
More beautiful than the softest kiss,
The miracle that returns each year,
Despite the violence, the bomb, the fear.

Patricia Mary Clark

WEST YORKSHIRE

What does West Yorkshire mean to me?
Friendly folk and cups of tea.
The very best of fish and chips,
Working men's clubs and seaside trips.
Bustling cities, quaint market places,
Ilkley Moor and wide open spaces.
Well kept allotments with veg and flowers
Where retired people spend many hours.
Homing pigeons, flapping tracks,
Men walking whippets and wearing flat caps.
Breathtaking scenery, walks in the dales.
Old fashioned sweet shops with polished brass scales.
Saturday afternoon weddings when strangers will wait
For a glimpse of the bride and groom at the church gate.
Pubs with a bowling green out at the back.
Rugby league football with tough men in the pack.
Back to back houses sparkling and neat
On either side of a cobble stoned street.
Whitsuntide walks when kids have new clothes,
The symbol of the Yorkshire Rose.
Very outspoken people who call a spade a spade,
The rag and bone mans cry as he plies his trade.
But the one special thing that makes me feel good
Is Mums' Sunday roast beef with Yorkshire pud!
You can keep your bungalows by the sea,
West Yorkshire is the place for me.

Ivy Singer

AUNTS ON PARADE - OR A YORKSHIRE WEDDING

It war' our Deirdre's wedding day and 'tposh plans 'ad been made,
The bride were dressed in fine array - and so were the bridesmaid.
The service ower, the photo's took, 'twer time for't weddin feast,
The bridegroom's mam were in a flap because 'er dress 'ad creased.

Our Deirdre's mam were clad in cream, accessories were pink,
They matched the colour of 'er eyes, she 'adn't slept a wink.
The best man made a *wicked* speech, it 'ad 'em all bent double,
Our Deirdre's Dad's 'ad bored 'em stiff, it wasn't worth the trouble.

All't aunts were out in fullest force, tongues sharp as sherry glasses,
The uncles paid no 'eed o' course, they eyed up all the lasses.
Relatives from ivery corner of our sovereign land
Came and looked and ate and supped and said 'Well in't this grand?'

The day wore on, the evening came, a disco 'ad been 'ired,
Someone took great Aunt Bertha 'ome, she were ninety-five - and
    tired.
Uncle Albert, on the other 'and were boppin' wi' the best,
'E were nobbut a lad o' seventy-nine and 'e didn't need a rest.

The beer ran out, the evening looked as though it might turn flat,
The bridegroom turned a pale green shade - and Aunt Beatrice lost
    'er 'at.
The pageboy pulled the bridesmaid's 'air, 'e paid fer this trick dearly,
She did karate twice a week and got medals for it yearly.

The bridegroom passed out quietly, ignored in the 'ub-bub,
All't aunts assembled on parade - and all't uncles in the pub.

Janette Meek

ODD SHAPED HILLS

Odd shaped hills, rolling dales,
Beautiful dry stone walls,
Purple brooding secret moors
Tarns and waterfalls.
Blackend mills, weaving sheds,
Pits and quarries closed,
Bronte's hockneys, colourful people
Talents undisclosed.

Barbara Grice

WHAT YORKSHIRE MEANS TO ME

A regular visitor from South to North
Yorkshire calls with such great force
Sights, there are many and all are just fine
Emmerdale, Heartbeat and Last of the Summer Wine
Museums, castles and grand stately homes
Gardens, Caves, Rocks, Rivers and Stones

Knaresborough holds a special place in my heart
The first time I visited, I felt I was part
Of that lovely old town with the river and boats
For somewhere to live, it would get all my votes

The Minster is seen from all over York
A wonderful view from the Walls as you walk
Quaint little shops in a narrow street
The Shambles is loved by all that she greets
To go into Betty's for tea and a cake
Is one visit I am compelled to make

A walk on the Moor through purple heather
The views are a joy whatever the weather
On you walk, no loos, no 'phones
In the middle, the Apostle Stones

Miles and miles of dry stone walls
The splash of water at Aysgarth Falls
The beauty, the splendour of those Yorkshire Dales
The peace, the tranquillity, it never fails
To give that feeling of being at home
And so many friends, you are never alone

Yorkshire pudding filled with gravy and meat
So big the portions, more than you can eat
And, never a problem with getting to sleep
After counting all those hundreds of sheep.

Irene Taylor

LEE GAP FAIR

Tomorrow will be fair day
No wonder I can't sleep
I'm feeling that excited
From the window I'll just peep

The horses will all be coming
Caravans will soon be here
With all the travelling people
That come this way each year

There'll be stalls all selling saddles
Brass's, leather straps, everything horses need
Roast chestnuts and toffee apples
Brandy snap, have a good feed

A man was chained up and put in a sack
I never thought He'd get out
He wriggled on his back, the chains dropped off
He jumped out and gave a loud shout

Men ran up the field with their horses
Showing them off, hoping for a sale
They gave a shout for folk to look out
Then they ran back down the field again

Dealers who were selling horses
Men who wanted to buy, or trade
Gave a shake of the hand to seal the deal
Many a good bargain was made

Something here for everyone
It comes round every year
Three weeks and three days to *Latter Lee*
We'll enjoy them both never fear.

Peggy Hunter

YORKSHIRE MOORS

A patchwork quilt of green and purple pink,
Winding pathways the sky to link.
Greystone houses set alone,
Adding warmth to the tone.
Telegraph poles intruding, stand aloft,
A welcome lifeline to a worker's croft.
Dry stone walls withstanding nature's worst,
Seeming to challenge winter's burst.
A swirl of mist cold and damp,
To make the walkers feet to stamp.
Sheep grazing upon the slope,
Dwelling perhaps on spring time hope.
Sparkling streams cool and bright,
Rippling o're stones washed smooth and white.
Upon the summit a snow white cap,
And north winds around the whole doth wrap.
Seasons changing the sun now high,
Brown the bracken, brittle dry.
Now hoards of people once more walking,
All winter of the moors were talking.
Who is there can resist nature's store,
As pathways beckon man once more?
An emerald set in Yorkshire's crown,
Complement your majestic gown.

Jean Venables

A MINER'S ADVICE TO HIS SON

So it's mining that you've chosen mylad, that comes a trifle thick
When we've given you an education, but you'd rather wield a pick.
Well you've got a lot of muscle and you'll want a lot of heart
And you'll need to don your thirsting togs, before you make a start.
I'd had my share of shifts below, a struggling in the black
With sweat awash my eyeballs and trickling down my back.

And the fire that your a-making, costs more than pounds and pence
What's on your dustpan's shovelled from a load of common sense.

How my heart was full of longing when my chops were full of dust
For the sweetness of the Lord's fresh air, above that tunnelled crust.
For the mercy of the blue sky, on a pair of weary eyes
Or the softness of the green grass, on a body's aching thighs.

Am I making you afraid then with this talk of all that's bad
Well there's lots of compensation down the bogey to be had.
You'll be working with real men, the salt of the earth
They'll teach you how to cuss, and take the p . . . for all their worth.

They'll brag about their conquests, their soccer and their darts
But you'll never want for nought lad if they take you to their hearts.
You have never heard the miners sing beneath the trembling earth
You know nothing about music as those angels know it's worth.

So here's my old pit helmet, if you look inside it lad
There's a heartache from your Mother and a blessing from your Dad.
We have told you all we can lad, there's nothing more to tell
So whatever you decide in life, go forth and do it well.

Fred Lunn

A SOUTHERNER'S POINT OF VIEW

Have you ever met a society that
will pass the time of day?
Try walking out of your home and
meeting friendly people on the way.
They may speak blunt they may be
bold in all they do and say,
but the West Yorkshire people are
always welcoming and have a cheery way.

Evelyn Tranter

CIRCA YORK

These Yorkshire wolds, and dales, tha' knows,
Match wi the best where ere tha goes,
In all the world. Maybe not in sun,
but for scenery, grub, and down reet fun!
It's all here. And there's history too
For them with nostalgic point of view.
They told him walk, so walk we do,
O'er moor and dale the whole year through,
We watch the pheasants, born and bred,
To die with buckshot in their head,
And ma'y's the deer that's jumped the hedge,
Where country lane nears woodland edge.
Then there's the sheep, and lambing days,
Early in t' year, and bridle ways,
Churned up with horses, a quagmire,
Where aconites and snowdrops flower,
And York has that which fine towns have,
All things to buy, a brand new lav,
Accommodations by the score,
To welcome tourists ever more.
Theatres, films, night clubs, the lot,
A hospital that's on the spot,
Especially for hearts,
Fine cremo for the dear departs,
These Yorkshire wolds, and dales, tha' knows,
Match wi the best where e'er tha goes,
Rose window in the Minister's grand,
Quiet reflection of the land,
That's Yorkshire.

Jean Heaven

SWAN SONG

Bradford's Swan Arcade surreal
once nestled in the navel
giving shelter from the rain
and goods for our appraisal
Swan Arcade beloved landmark
never more to grace the scene
still lives in memory serene.

Lattice arches cast in iron
by men with surnames like O'Brien
poured into moulds by Ron and Ted
their faces permanently red
at end of shift they slaked their thirst
but made it back to work the first.
One man could not beat the clock
Dennis missed the gates that locked.

Now usurped by welded steel
must we mourn the lost surreal
or shall their likes again resurge
and as from welded steel emerge
into sturdy webs of scrolls and twirls?

Should men of long ago artistic
They made the Swan Arcade so mystic
see the new age spandrels plain
its surly anger they'd return
our Swan Arcade to resurrect it.
God shield us from their faces
not red but bright red apoplectic.

Charles Maries

OUR YORKSHIRE BITS

From Flamborough Head to Whitby's fame,
No two pleasures quite the same.
The ups and downs of Cleveland Way
and perfect sweep of Robin Hood's Bay.

Rabbit, pheasant, a song bird's trills,
The coarse debate of Scalby Mills.
The Regal Lady lost in fog,
Beach notice saying 'Ban the dog.'

Peasholm's trees;- so much splendour,
Drunken yobbos on a bender,
A gated road where nature's clever,
Wild orchids first, then grouse and heather.

The hoi polloi of village shows,
The quiet white of winter's snows,
Stately homes, abbeys, country park,
Sunsets fading into dark.

Forge Valley, Hackness, river's bend,
New Year's Eve at Langdale End,
Thornton Dale via Forest Drive,
Refresh at The Buck; you'll survive.

Sutton Bank and fair Maybeck,
Elusive deer; no 'ee by heck.'
We've seen trains 'smoke and heard their hiss,
So many tourists thronged for this.

Perhaps they came and maybe sat,
At view points shown upon a map,
To gaze at forest, moor and dale,
Perhaps they know a Yorkshire tale.

E Bell

YORKSHIRE MOORS

Just sit awhile just relax
In this countryside, we know best.
What do you feel, at ease at last?
Go out on the moors
In the bracken and heather.
How peaceful you feel, forgetful of weather.
Just walk so slow, you are on your own.
This beauty all around you.
Miles from home.
The running streams all around.
No fencing here to be found.

Be so quiet, you might see the deer,
Just listen awhile, and feel what you hear.
The frogs are croaking, the bees are there too.
Enjoying the heather to make.
Honey for you and for me.
The pheasant, and crows strutting around.
Thinking they are safe, while on the ground.
On movement from you
They are off in a flash.
Don't you worry, they will come back.

The smell of the heather, just lets you know.
This is God's country, that is so.
From the grime and dirt, that we see.
If we could take, the young and old.
Let them see, the beauty, to unfold.
Make this life a happier place.
And to love one another
Is not out of place.

Agnes Solan

EXILE

Oh, I'm home again in Yorkshire,
And I'll never leave again,
For I've been too long in exile,
Where there's nothing worth the gain,
There, the seeking of ambition,
Through the mythic streets of gold
Found the people and the places
Held an emptiness untold.
There the shops and cars and houses,
And the theatres and schools,
Spoke a strange and foreign language
With a set of cryptic rules.
Here the country folk are faithful
And the sun shines in their smile,
The words they speak are honest,
In their hearts I'll find no guile.
I shall walk upon the hilltops,
Where peace lies over all.
Or follow through the valleys
Where I'll hear the rivers call.
I'll be here once more in Springtime
When the daffodils are gold,
And in August when the heather
Cloaks the Dales in purple fold.
I shall be here for ever,
And I'll never go away,
For my heart belongs to Yorkshire
So this is where I'll stay.

Yes, my heart belongs to Yorkshire.
And this is where I'll stay.

Eileen Walters

UNSIGHTED

How soft the air caresses my cheek
On summery nights of holiday week,
A week I usually spend by the sea
As I let the ozone invigorate me
To give me strength and make we well
So I can work harder and able to sell
My produce and wares in the coming year
They are not cheap nor are they dear
I start at eight and work till five thirty
My job is not what one might term dirty
But I would give pounds could I but see
My finished products just as they be
But alas this cannot be done
For I am blind, and I am just one
Of many thousands in this sorry plight
Where days are always as dark as night
But I thank God for what I hold
Things that are much more precious than gold
I can taste, hear, smell and feel by touch
To normal people this may not seem much
But as water's not missed till the well runs dry
Babies faces you don't miss seeing until you try
That's one of the times when you may feel sad
And cheer yourself by saying I must be mad
To grumble at my small infirmity
For when I'm in heaven then shall I see
As He will restore my sight to me
He'll give me success, and power to trust
In His loving goodness forever I must.

T E Armitage

I THE HUMBER BRIDGE

I, The Humber Bridge stand tall, with a lovely view of fields
and villages all around - the ships and a windmill too,
The trains pass by with people travelling to and fro,
Everywhere in winter time are coverings of snow.

I've caused a great sensation, the news has passed all round,
'Do you know that bridge my dear, has cost over one hundred
                                        and sixty million pounds?'
I'm very proud to stand here, so fine, so big and tall,
I'm the only one around, who can overlook you all.

I see both sides of Humberside, with hearts so fine and true,
The City of Hull is old you see, whilst I am only new,
I'm nearly ready for my work, to stand the tide of wear,
Maybe someone nice will say a tiny little prayer.

For me the Bridge, who will be here, for many and many a year,
I know that when I'm christened, I'll shed a little tear,
The workers who have built me, so fine, so big and tall,
May I say a little word, 'Yes, God Bless you all.'

They've dressed me up so lovely, especially at night,
The lights that are placed on me are such a beautiful sight,
I can be seen for miles around, I feel so great, so new,
I even peep behind the trees, to have a look at you.

Soon the crowds will visit me, I'm waiting with delight,
I am the Bridge, and you will know . . . I'm such a wondrous sight,
The ribbon's cut, the champagne flows and I stand proud over
                                          the River below,
So fine, so big, so tall and proud . . . I the Humber Bridge, am
                                          alive, you should know
so when you pass over . . . please say 'Hello.'

V Aston

MY TOWN

Huddersfield - West Yorkshire,
The town of the comedians' jokes.
But no matter where you travel,
You won't find better folks.

Hard working, down to earth, that's us,
Cries of help are always heeded.
A sense of humour, a listening ear
Sometime is all that's needed.

Our famous worsted cloth
Is made in mills right here.
But sadly things are in decline,
Due to cheap imported gear.

Film star, Prime Minister, business tycoon,
This town has produced all three.
Their faces known all over the world,
Fame and success for all to see.

The hills, the fields, the dry stone walls,
Are just the artist's dream.
So if the stress of life gets hold
Come up here and let off steam.

Up high on our lovely moors
Strange objects have started to appear.
Wind turbines, they are called
Cheap energy to make we hear.

West Yorkshire has so much to offer,
Why not come and take a look?
You'll find it better in real life
Than from the pages of a book.

Phyllis Mosley

THE BUTTRESS BLUES

The Buttress winds down to Hebden bridge Town,
From Heptonstall high in the hills
But with weed it is choked, the path we once walked,
As we went to our work in the mills.

But some how I fear it will never be clear
Because no one will tackle the job.
The council won't pay, 'cause it's not a highway,
And they know it will cost a few bob.

On the Buttress I knew, no grass ever grew,
It was trampled to death from the start
for the sewing shop lasses, put paid to the grasses,
(And there's still some around that took part).

Each day they ran down to work in the town,
The never ran back, you can bet.
And the hand rail so trusty, it never went rusty.
It was oiled every day by their sweat.

And the clatter of clogs, in the mist and the fogs
Of the smoke filled valley was heard
And as things went to seed, be it grass tree or weed
It was crushed before growth had occurred.

Now the work has all gone, and the tourists have come,
They all travel by car or by bus.
Once bare as a bone it is now overgrown.
And the council is making a fuss.

If they want those times back, everybody from Slack,
Hepton and Blackhawhead too,
Stop using your motors, buy clogs for your daughter
And walk it, as we used to do.

W H Metcalfe

YORKSHIRE BRED

Born on the Pennines in June '71,
My birthplace was *Saddleworth* by name,
The county was Yorkshire - which meant nothing then,
But soon did as my later years came.

In '74 our boundaries were changed,
Greater Manchester's where we were placed,
I didn't mind then - but I was only three,
Now I think it's a total disgrace!

For as I've grown older, I've learnt about pride,
And the bond between *Tykes* everywhere,
And though I've now moved, I still long for the day,
When the white rose again blossoms there.

Since '82 I've called Scarborough my home,
Where I came every year as a child,
Compared to the moors it's a bustling place,
And the winters are usually mild.

All through my teens I played cricket of course,
As every young Yorkshireman should,
But take my advice - don't chase *county caps*,
If like me, you're not really that good!

These days what riles me, above anything else,
Is when people think I come from *Lancs*,
I say - Just 'cos me folks come from t'wrong side of t'hills,
Don't mean that 'ar do - no thanks!'

See, I'm proud of my county - a beautiful land,
With warm people and such history,
And wherever I go, there's one thing I can't change,
I'm from Yorkshire - and always shall be!

Ryan Bartram

NIGEL'S GHOST

Fed up with the endless darkness
and his boils playing up each day
prompted a restless spirit
to abscond from his bed of clay

His life had been filled with laughter
as he held and taught ladies to dance
tempting Vera might still be there waiting
alas not the ghost of a chance

He set off for the coast and Blackpool
for a dip and a change of air
the recession had been there before him
and left it quite empty and bare

He had nautical blood (when he had some)
so went fishing for cod which he craved
but the ship went down in a hurricane
and he was the only one saved

Taking the road to the highlands
he nipped into a shop for a kilt
for he knew that the breeze in the Cairngorms
might cause his old bull's - eye to wilt

At last he was sure of a welcome
in the valley's, the towns and the pits
but he found himself holding a placard
Home rule for Aberystwyth.

He gave up and returned to the graveyard
where at least it was peaceful and quiet
except for the dogs and the pigeons
and developers hoping to buy it.

James C Goff

WINTER BLEAK IN HEPTONSTALL

The scene from my bedroom window was diffused with fluffy snow,
Distant cottages were ghostlike peering through the falling flow.
The majestic trees of summer green,
Are laden in white winter sheen.

I left my cosy dwelling and trod the virgin snow.
The lively thud on stone flag was compressed to muffled slow.
The snowflakes touch upon my cheek,
Increased the chill of winter bleak.

The dwellings on the narrow track seem ominous today,
Their greyness of the previous day in darkest black array.
Each consumed in lifeless stance,
Glowing gloom as snowflakes dance.

No cats lay snug on window sill, no frisky dogs astir,
No robin redbreasts cheery trill to break the silent blurr.
No greetings of 'Hello, *Adieu*,'
To warm the icy blast of winter's rue.

The crunch of footsteps on the snow do frighten me today,
Consumed in winter silence, they add to my dismay,
I was glad to leave the village to walk the wastes of snow,
To see the snowflakes falling to the valley down below.

I slowly trod to Hebden Town,
Where winter bleak did not there frown.
Where oppressive silence melted, just like the fallen snow,
And the thud of footsteps on the flags, replaced the muffled slow.

Stuart Marriott

MARKET DAY

'Come buy my fresh vegetables.' You hear the men calling.
You've coins in your pocket, and you've come to buy.
Fresh greens for your dinner, cabbage, leeks and potatoes,
'I can't make my mind up.' You think, with a sigh.

Rosy apples, and oranges, bananas, and grapefruit,
Tomatoes, and lettuce, and salad is here,
heaped up, on the barrows, and stalls, and in boxes.
'It's your choice lady, and nothing is dear.'

Here are ironmongers, and clothiers, and florists, fish,
Household equipment, and paint for the walls.
Pots and pans, crockery, lines, and pegs for your washing,
Children's toys, and handbags, all laid out on the stalls.

This then, is the market, thriving, and bustling.
Set on the cobbles of most Yorkshire towns.
It's lovely, to shop there, on a spring day, or in summer,
as you walk through the crowds, in fresh air, from the downs.

Farmers bring cattle, poultry, and rabbits,
Selling and buying, it's all part of their lives,
and there's always a stall, of fresh butter, and cheeses,
produced with skill, and patience, by their busy wives.

I love a market, the bustle, and the laughter,
Mothers call their children, to stay at their side,
If I save enough money, I'll go there this weekend,
The atmosphere's great, and range of goods very wide.

There's so much to see, local characters. And friendships.
People I meet, every week, going down.
I relax, and feel happy, when I've browsed round our market.
For it's all a way of living, in our lovely Yorkshire towns.

Dawn England

FILEY

From Scarborough through to Brid.,
The golden coast is hid,
The Brigg, the hills and fields,
Its hidden treasures yield,
The castles and the mounds, a history abounds,
The smugglers and the caves,
The freedom of the slaves,
The far reaching sea, the fish at bay,
The Cobble Landing of today,
The fishermen and wives,
The coastguard saving lives,
The lifeboat sails both day and night,
Through peril, sway and plight,
The lighthouse white and tall,
Shines to warn us all,
The dangers of the sea,
The sunken ships and war's U-boats,
Wrecked upon the deep seabed,
Memories of old and victorious dead,
The wars were won but blood was shed,
The past has gone, the future ahead,
Historians, geologists, archaeologists descend,
The evidence within, the mysteries end,
Environmentalists and conservationists too,
Fight pollution on land and in the sea for you,
Twitchers come and search the skies,
Off Bempton Cliff the rare bird flies,
Traders come with market stalls,
Tourists come for fun and all,
By road and rail and sea.

Lorraine Robertshaw

DALBY FOREST

North Yorkshire has picturesque jewels
splendid, spacious and green.
A trip through paths in the forest
show Dalby tall and serene.
The conifers there are high, wide and handsome
nature's treasures for all to behold
as the sun spreads its rays through the treetops,
to the green, add a touch of pure gold.
Areas are there for a picnic
carved benches and tables for all
Freedom abounds for the children together
For the lean and the lanky, the small and the tall.
Off they head for the corner, all playful
the noise can be deafening as thunder.
As they clamber around having great fun
up-down-in-out-over-through and under.
There's a small, winding stream,
so pleasant and peaceful
walk by with maybe a stop;
and eventually strive to carefully arrive
at the interesting heritage shop.
A chart on the wall for viewers to see
one look and you'll soon catch the thread
of forest achievements, worked in the past
new plans for the years lying ahead
as you take with you happy contentment
a smile on everyone's face,
it's always nice to remember
Dalby Forest is a beautiful place.

Mary L Burton

WEST YORKSHIRE

The hills and dales of Yorkshire
Are the treasures of my mind,
Wherever I go, in sun or snow,
No lovelier place I'll find.

Forget the hills and slag heaps,
That used to spoil the view,
Most are gone, their work is done,
Green fields bring hopes anew.

Let's sing the praises of Yorkshire,
Let everybody know, let's tell
We're not just flat caps and braces,
We've got other things as well.

I'm proud of my Yorkshire dialect
That tells the place of my birth,
No need to trace my folks or race,
I'm Yorkshire that proves my worth.

So come, you southern cousins,
Visit our county so fair,
See our hills, and seas, our moors and trees,
And warm-hearted folks everywhere.

Then tell of all the things you've seen
The places you most admire,
The country inns, the friendly grins,
You find throughout the shire.

So let the name of Yorkshire
Mean something good and true,
And as we are proud of Yorkshire,
Let Yorkshire be proud of you.

Mary Reynolds

THE MILL

In the days of long ago,
To the mills they used to go,
Where the wool was stacked in bales -
Old folk tell of all these tales.

Rising early in the day,
Through the fog they'd make their way,
Quietly in droves they went,
Work for them was heaven sent.

Then machines began to roll,
Many times health took the toll,
Although the folk had lots of grit,
They really needed to be fit.

Lunch would be just bread and jam,
If they were *posh*, it could be *spam*,
But most folk didn't have much cash,
So tea was often meat and *mash*.

An old tin bath afore the fire
Soothed aching bodies work did tire,
Then before the firelight's glow
They'd sit with wives who liked to sew.

Sometimes they would sing a song
To help the long, dark nights along.
To bed - the clothes dropped to the floor.
And then there'd be a mighty snore.

Soon the dawn would come around,
And they'd be off without a sound.
At the mill gates they'd all throng,
And soon t'machines would roll along.

Margaret Hooper

SCOUTING FOR MOTHERS

I will show you, he said
where our mountain bikes
plunged and laboured over stones
forced, swerved between boulders.
I will take you in bright sunlight
where, on a wet November day
we were lost. Voices close
in the stillness of mist, our breath
thickened grey dissolving walls
wet, blank as a mapless page
until a boot stumbling found the path
and we were safe;
at home, you never knew.

I will show you where we climbed
straining and scrabbling
crabbing and gasping
muscles high-wired and stinging with pain
we reached for the table-edge
and the sky above it.
Yes, like them. They scarcely move
and the ledges are white with chalk.

A sprig of heather for you!
I know this country
like you know your garden
but differently. I know
where to find shelter
and where a pillow of snow lies longest
and the bit that's always boggy, sucking;
or dry, like brown underfelt
that powders our boots with cocoa
Good soil, this, for growing boys.

Hilary Shields

ME DAD

Me dad, he was a Yorkshire lad,
his life was hard, but not so bad;
he lived within a cottage small,
on Oxenhope Moor 'longside a wall.
His dad cut peat to make the fire,
for wintertime was cold and dire.
When t'fire smoked and made a pother,
they'd clean up t'chimley - one way or t'other.
They'd take a bunch of heather twig,
a rope, a stone (it must be big).
Then t'chimley cleaning got agate,
with heather on t'rope, and stone as weight.
On t'roof went dad - his dad inside -
for heights his dad could not abide.
Down the t'chimley now t'contraption went,
to clear out t' soot was its intent.
And then with t'soot all swept away,
and t' fire relit at t' end of t'day,
with watter fetched from t'deep, cold well,
into a cauldron for a spell.
O'er t' fire to make it warm enough,
to have a wash - for soot's black stuff!
When clean again and t' oil lamp lit,
it seemed like time to eat a bit -
some oatcake, cheese; and good, thick stew,
and so to truckle bed, and then,
when t' cock crew - time for up again!

Aye me dad, he was a Yorkshire lad,
and I'm a Yorkshire lass mes'en!

Jean M Senior

A WALK IN YORKSHIRE

Walking is a lovely pastime
even when it's freezing.
Who would miss a gorgeous treat
that leaves you cold and sneezing?
In thermal undies, woolly jerseys
good thick trews and mitts
Pom-pom hats, mohair scarves
and anything warm that fits.
We plod along the frozen paths
the puddles solid ice
what else could we be doing
that's nearly quite as nice?
The wind has turned my face all blue
I suppose it could be duller
but I don't mind, for as it happens
blue is my favourite colour.
The fields are bare, I stand and stare
but not for long I found
for if I did I am sure my feet
would freeze onto the ground.
I remove my gloves to eat my snack
my hands are now in sight
they go pale blue to match my face
I think it's called frostbite.
Four miles to go it started snowing
the depth of snow just grew and grew
I wish that I was safe back home
I have never built an igloo.
The scenery I will remember forever
this Yorkshire land, I will leave you, never.

Judith M Rudge

UNTITLED

Bradford used to be grimy and mucky
with cobbles which rattled with clogs,
olde worlde pubs and some kind of clubs
where fellas would meet for a pint,
the stalls in town were open late,
with things sold off on the cheap,
horses with carts, men selling their wares
were part of the bygone scene,
but now take a look at our *Bradford*
our lovely tourist town.
We have shops in stores, markets indoors
and shops with prices knocked down,
we have bargains through the charity chains
we have theatre and cinema too,
we can even call at a coffee shop and
ask for, 'Tea for two!'
Though Bradford is a tourist town, with
a beautiful city hall,
we have lovely parks and floral displays
museums which cater for all,
we have art and pleasure in many ways
at our treasured Cartwright Hall.
Gone are the days of misery when children
had to work hard, under machines
tidying knots and rats running round
in the yard.
I'm proud to belong to *Bradford*,
a Yorkshire tyke at heart,
and anything that's going on,
I like to play my part.

Shirley Harrison

MY PENNINE ROOTS

I'm proud to be a Yorkshire lass
My feelings never roam,
No other town can quite surpass . . . .
My Calder valley home.

Close communal family life
Feuds are very rare,
Stern and strong in times of strife,
Troubles they can share.

Plans did not fail -
A change or two,
Where once stood a jail . . .
A road runs through!

Such ruthless news,
Bestowed on the town
Mills and mews . . .
Came tumbling down.

Gone were the days,
Of cobbles and sets
Up rose a maze . . .
Of the *maisonettes*.

The church of St Mary
Continues to stand
Designers were wary . . .
To keep off her land!

Though Elland, has altered
Been put to the test,
My thoughts haven't faltered,
It's by far - the best.

Catherine Howard

THE SILENT LOOMS

An invite to lunch at the in-place, Salts Diner.
To eat salt beef on rye, also fast food cuisine, none finer!
I laugh as I accept, we're here in Saltaire, Shipley, Yorkshire,
Not downtown New York, uptown Chicago or even Carolina!
I'm neither sceptical or cynical, simply a Yorkshire lass, down
                                                                    to earth,
OK. I'd go, if only to see the Hockney's on display at their gallery
I could do a lot worse, old stick in the mud, me!
The day was cold, I'd heard of the vastness of the rooms,
Would there be ghosts still weaving on the old now silent looms?
The magnificent building stands twixt railway, canal and road,
Sir Titus a canny man placed it strategically, Salts Mill,
Goods easy to load and more importantly, offload!
A shock to my eager eyes! The vastness, the milling throng,
                                                         some browsing,
Others pondering, passing comment on the local lads'
                                          prowess, carousing.
The lady in the plastic rainhood stared at his life-size photo, sighed,
'He's got a big 'ole in 'is pullover and I'm sure 'is 'air's dyed!'
The looms are silent, the mills not as before, no clacking of bobbins,
As huge speakers pipe arias from a famous Puccini score,
Walls bedecked with vibrant colours, the old mill's transformation,
Would Sir Titus turn in his grave? I think he'd applaud,
This Leeds lad, Jonathan Silver, saved it from demolition,
From being ravaged stone by stone, when dispatched cruelly aboard!
Generations apart these two entrepreneurs, but not so different,
                                                             why?
Both businessmen, devout, caring for the place, somewhat shy?
Me, I've never wanted to be in with the in-crowd, hating glamour
                                                       and glitz.
Never desired a hamper from Harrods, or to dine at the Ritz!
I leave Salts Mill stomach full, feeling nostalgic, happy at heart.
Forgetting the FT Index, the news, talk of impending gloom
My mind is still full of Hockney bold ventures, colours and success.
I'm grateful to those silent looms as I reluctantly depart.

Joyce Hefti Whitney

A DREAM FULFILLED

For many a year - yes, many a year,
I wandered far over land and sea
while fairer prospects lured me on
and home was where I happened to be.
Yet, I held a memory close to my heart
of Yorkshire's moors spreading wide and free
and the music I heard was the voice of the wind
singing sweet litanies for me.

I remembered a city deep-rooted in time,
misted in dreams of long ago,
where ghostly bowmen man the walls,
stand guard against a long-dead foe;
and a cathedral, centuries old,
towering above an ancient street,
spires reaching for the stars,
flagstones worn by a million feet.

'Twas many a year - yes, many a year
since last I breathed my native air
and heard the sound of the Minster bells
calling York citizens to prayer.
Beneath the heat of alien skies
I dreamed of the land where I belong;
of the crisp, cold purity of snow and,
in the spring, the blackbird's song . . .

I could not have said when
      but I promised then
           that, someday, my steps
                would turn homeward again . . .

Anne Isobel Dawson

THE PLACE FOR ME

I live in a city in Yorkshire
I'm an old fashioned Yorkshire lass
and I wouldn't want to swap places
not for any amount of brass

This city of ours is right famous
I don't have to mention name
all I needs is United
and soccer's name of game

I've a park that's a pleasure to walk in
it's grand, just like in books
we like having picnics on lakeside
and we saves all are crust to feed ducks

We're two minutes ride from country
where there's tree and flowers and grass
we're same distance from town centre
where we goes she we wants to spend brass

West Yorkshire folk are right friendly
we like a laugh and a joke
and as we all say in Yorkshire
you won't find 'owt wrong wi right folk

Some folk would say that I'm bias
well with that I might just agree
there's no nicer place what to live in
West Yorkshire's the place for me.

Elizabeth Ryan

YORKSHIRE YEAR

When snow not only falls but freezes on the trees
And branches dip on either side of narrow lanes
We may complain but have we not been also blessed
By fairy grottoes dressed like Christmas stores
And moorland vistas inspiring as the sea?

Then winter sunshine glints from mirrors on the moors
That could be water but when you climb
Are flattened snowdrifts substantial in their time
Now oozing beads to becks through soggy fields
That yield a feast for threescore visiting redwings.

And even now above the snow
Rehearsing songs our own birds watch in turn
To see which yearning stems that now seem bare
Will speck with green this year and show them how
Their nests may best and safely soon be hidden.

And long before town gardeners announce their spring
The sun on untrimmed hedge and woodland verge
Will urge from twigs unharmed by frosted grips of snow
A light-reflecting show of hawthorn's palms
And curling woodbine's pale, soft spears.

No sharp divisions mark as human fictions do
The subtle shifting scene that Yorkshire's guardians share
With careworn year-round guests who in their thousands choose
The soothing balm that views and boundless wendings give
To those who live in crowds with thoughts of endings.

All summer wood and headland flowers many snatch our gaze
But then a blaze of purple takes the prize
And calls our eyes to where the sky and heather meet
Entreating us to heed that queer unearthly thought
That brought us here in search of England's birth.

John Keeble

CATHEDRAL GRAVES

The city dwellers
Walk over words
Reading *Here Lies* and
Beloved and dated
Long gone.

The road works
Dig through them
And bombs
Were dropped on them
And seasons
Blow past them,
But they never change.

The courting walked round them
To wait on Cole's Corner
And choristers
Laugh
And don't notice they're there.

The dead city dwellers
Staying in heaven
Just shiver at times.
If we could ask them
Why they appeared so cold
They would say,
'Why, someone down there's just
Walked over my grave.'
So think on, when you walk
Over those long-laid stones
That someone is shivering,
But safe from your footsteps.

Kate Ibbeson

A FAVOURITE PLACE

The boys' laughter echoes between crevices
of rising ruggedness.
Below, the gurgling shallows flow.
With gentle urgency they ripple
across rainbow stones.
Made smooth by paddling feet.

The spring sunlight glimmers, making dancing
partners of trunk and branch.
They leafily sway over the deep pool.
Straw longboats begin their hazardous race,
spinning and gliding under the wooden bridge.
At the end they lie a soddened mass,
defeated.

The opposing grassy bank nurtures
the hungry ewe.
With wary eyes, she now protects her
crying offspring.
Together they climb through footpaths of green fern.
To escape the human intrusion.

The seasons pursue.
Soft purple carpets unfold,
undulating to the horizon.
Following, the grey threatening sky
shows black silhouettes.
Winter white has enveloped and silenced.
The Moors sleep.

Jean Leathley

THE MINSTER: YORK

Here I stand, and scarcely can I move
As I gaze aloft towards heaven's roof,
For I'm struck with awe as mine eyes meet
The splendour before me in the street,

For here a mighty cathedral rises
Above the chimneytops of houses,
And over office-blocks and shops -
It seems that the masonry never stops!

It's almost too much for human eyes
To absorb the great breathtaking size,
I feel as small as a tiny mouse
As I look upon this sacred house!

Three towers ascend from the mountain of stone,
Two to the west and a central one, alone.
Turrets and spires appear everywhere -
A congregation it seems, assembled for prayer!

Mullioned windows are spaced across the wall
But the beautiful *rose* outshines them all,
Ornamental pinnacles crown the cathedral -
This lovely church built in times medieval.

A man-made miracle is this holy place
Raised to the glory of God's good grace,
Angels must surely look down from above
And bless this majestic labour of love.

Joyce Atkinson

JOIN US FOR A BEER

Welcome to South Yorkshire
Come in, there's lots of room -
Vast, wide-open spaces
Derelict now, no traces
Of a great industrial boom.

But we're proud of our heritage:
Castles, manors, halls,
Museums, priories, churches,
Abbeys with graceful arches -
Past deeds safe within their walls.

A favourite pastime's shopping,
You can spend your brass round here:
There's Meadowhall - stupendous!
Retail World - tremendous!
You'll go home broke I fear.

How about a trip to the Arena
Where famous stars are seen:
Neil Diamond, UB40,
Dire Straits and Pavarotti
And skaters Torvill and Dean.

If sport is what you fancy
There's lots to watch or play:
Soccer, cycling, yachting,
Cricket, swimming, putting
Or golf will make your day.

So welcome to South Yorkshire,
You'll find a deal of cheer:
Let's forget the current recession,
Dole queues and depression -
Come and join us for a beer!

Dorothy Shaw

TANKERSLEY

The bats and owls no longer skim
the roof of the Norman church, as when we were young,
As the choir boys shuffled, and the final hymn
Of the evensong was sung.

Past the Bullwood and Willowgarth down the Black Lane,
Leading to the Old Hall, stark and gaunt,
Like a broken skeleton the fragments remain
For Cromwell's forgotten army to haunt.

The Ladies' Folly, now demolished, stood on a mound
Where men, long gone, dug for ironstone
Now members play golf on that undulating ground,
Where the battle of Tankersley was won.

The rectory and its garden, where fêtes were held and goods
                                                      displayed,
Close by the Glebe Farm and its *listed* pigeon cote,
Tadpoles and minnows, a green where children played,
A wall now surrounds the remnants of this ancient moat.

Across the fields lies Hangsman Stone Bar Farm,
From the name a legend, or is it fact, has begun;
Its stone barn and olde worlde charm,
Give credence to the yarn that both sheep and man were hung.

All local mines, Rockingham and Wharncliffe Silkstone
Have been replaced by opencast today,
The LNER and GC railway lines have also gone
A hindrance to the M1 motorway.

So strangers as you speed on your way,
We know not why or where,
As you contemplate tomorrow, consider yesterday,
Through South Yorkshire please drive with care.

W Ullyott

OUR CASTLE

Strong, silent sentinel, keep of stone
Historic castle, of defence grey to age
Matured to nature's mood, defied alone
Erect and proud, persevered stormy rage
Set in rock, man's folly to tolerate
Thy beauty breathes alive traditional scene
Thy vallum withstood, furious foe's all abate
The glory of Conisborough, thy presence redeem.

Designed of man, deemed forbidding cold
Thy crown seem kiss, unhurried white cloud
Old image now warm, ancient charm unfold
Perfect thy setting, yet mystery enshroud
In splendour reign thy panoramic rule
Ravaged in bygone war and confrontation
Arid thy moat, dancing trout once pool
Portals now ajar, doth welcome all nation.

Did *holy* being mark thy pleasant place
On mound aloof, to gaze on flowing don
Akin *Mill Piece,* nestles snug of verdant face
Rekindle our thoughts, of age long gone
Doth knight of past thy precinct's ghost
Thy greens full courts, amuse to jesters' fun
Our heritage preserved, town's birth you host
Then *pray* you stand, till death of sun.

Plantagenets and Tudors, thou did survive
Chronicled events, to thy record did chart
Plague of Black, and God's laws revised
Thou stood time's test, derelict and apart
How humble we stand, to stony might
thy silhouette outlined to beam of *moon*
Or thy monument, archives relate a noble plight
May future mankind, *thy existence 'ere groom.*

Benny Wilkinson

A BIT ABAH'T BARNSLEY

We've gor a dish in Barnsley,
They call it *Barnsley Chops,*
An if you've gor an appetite,
You'll think it is the tops.

We've other dishes as well
Of which you'll have heard lots of talk;
Abah't Albert Hirst's black puddings,
And his pies wots all full o' pork.

Nah Barnsley had a brewery
Wot brewed bitter as clear as a bell.
Ah could they do ony other -
When't water came straight from't Oak Well?

Town Hall is one't cleanest,
In fact it looks almost white;
They gave it a wash and brush up
When't new mayor were called *Mrs Bright.*

Open air market wer't biggest
'At folks in Yorkshire had seen;
Market Hill, Queen's Road, Gas Nook,
And 'specially - May Day Green.

We've got chaps in't market
What's famous thro' being seen on't TV
Like Joe Edwards at' pot stall -
Shows three days a week an' all free.

But nah we've gor a market hall
Where you ship and pay.
Alas we've lost the atmosphere
We once had . . . yesterday!

Roy Portman

FORGET THE DALES

There's more than tykes peculiar to Yorkshire.
There's Morley's rhubarb. Men force it to mature
squealing in low darkened sheds.
Once exported to France, it made
Champagne extending wine,
defying appellation.

Some sheds force mushrooms now.
Mycelium, boxed in peak-heated horse muck
covered with peat and chalk
through which in dim, warm silence
we can watch the fungus grow.

Still waiting for the final accolade -
Yorkshire pudding
would have been dubbed with Sir Loin of Beef
had Henry's chef
been born within the Ridings.

To help *you* make the perfect pudding
I am willing to say just this,
the secret is in the measuring.
Just the right amount of flour, of milk and egg to whisk,
but most of all the volume of the batter
poured into each square inch of searing dish.
When cooked, to this perfection add
gravy from the brisket.
There you have
A Yorkshire pudding starter.

Keith Stokes

TALE OF A YORKSHIRE HUBBY

She proudly pranced around the room, new hairdo and sweet perfume,
Television quietly grey, candles burning, end of day.
Enter husband, 'Quick, it's on, don't want dinner, hunger's gone,'
'Where's the kids, in bed, I hope?' 'Did you make our John use soap?'
Wifie sitting gnashing teeth, feels the need to buy a wreath,
Hubby's murder quite a shock, she'd end up sitting in the dock,
No that's no good, must think again, perhaps a trip down memory lane,
She cuddled close, 'Do you remember, a lonely beach, 'twas in September,'
'Shut up woman, watch the score, do some knitting or scrub the floor.
I must have my fill of sport, this coming season's much too short.'
She jumped up quick in angry rage, rattled the budgie inside its cage,
Ran around, did the splits, smashed the room into little bits,
Threw the dinner around the walls, took up squash with three meatballs,
Ripped up all the curtains twice, sprinkled the chairs in sugar and spice,
Whirled an axe in great, good measure, collapsed and sighed, she'd had her pleasure,
Hubby looked up from the set, 'It's gone off now, I've won my bet,
What was it you tried to say, it's been a lovely, quiet day.
This room's a bit untidy love, I'll bet the kids just haven't been good,
Never mind, tomorrow night, we'll watch again, boy what a sight!'

Annie Storey

A TEAR FOR THE MINERS

The pits are going one by one
2000 will see them all but gone
Communities in despair
Will come into media glare
His trademark was the grimy face
As he came up from that awful place
Our gold was rich and black
Hewn on knee and back
Miner if given chance
Will hope for a second glance
But the mines' fall from grace
Will surely bring a greener place
Winding, winding wheels
Contractors now doing deals
With pick and spade
A price had to be paid
Often through loss of life,
And led to grieving wife
Gas is now to be king
It has a somewhat hollow ring
All looks dishevelled
As pits, broken and levelled
Didn't there used to be a corner shop here
Someone says through glistening tear?
Now gone the old tin bath
Which must have heard many a laugh
A land fit for heroes
Now dependant on giros
Their skills now upon the heap
Forever there to sleep.

James Cann

RECOLLECTIONS OF BATELY (WEST YORKS)

Now in a busy Yorkshire town
where streets go up steep hills then down
there used to come from every street
much noise for clogs were on most feet

You'll find this town in Yorkshire (West)
it has a pleasant place to rest
a public park where everyone
can rest or have some jolly fun

This park's divided into two
a cafe that will welcome you
a children's playground, boating lake
if tired of these you then can take

Some upward paths you'll call a maze
in olden days these were a craze
and somewhere in those paths you'll find
a rest for feet, food for the mind

Two shelters and two poems that rhyme
that you can read if you have the time
out of this maze a house you'll see
to enter there 'tis not quite free

A room you'll call *the kitchen room*
although you see no pan or broom
a waxen lady in her chair
will surely make you stand and stare

A spinning-wheel before her hand
so lifelike this, it looks quite grand
and in the gloom you'll think it so
my mother did long years ago.

Rosamond Cox

YORKSHIRE

Near Ilkla Moor we used to live
Amid bracken we would play
Finding the secrets it wished to give
Where the things that made our day.

Rabbits so young they had no fur
Birdnests so beautiful, hidden around
We'd not touch them, that wouldn't be fair
Just a peek! Then leave them as found.

Oh! I wish that I was a young thing
As down to the farm I would go
To see the lass amilking
Oh! How I truly loved it so.

The bull calf would chase around
To hide behind her skirt
Afraid, he knocked me to the ground
And tread me in the dirt.

He is just like a wee wean
His mum, was what he was at
Soon back on his own again
The milkmaid saw to that.

Life is not always what it seems
When future beckons we go
Now I'm old, I'm left with my dreams
But that's not bad you know.

Muriel Jenkins

FROM NEW TO OLD

From new to old they came one day,
    To see the sights of York
And asked if we would show the way,
    As they began their walk.
Guy, in amazement, said, 'Gee whiz!'
    The Minster having seen
And heard that seven centuries,
    That building there had been.
Into the Minster then they went
    And wondered at the glass,
The knave and choir magnificent,
    Much did it all surpass.
The city walls did they ascend,
    Each view was a surprise.
To see the shambles was the end,
    Could they believe their eyes?
Medieval buildings, large and small,
    So quaint and full of charm,
In much delight, they captured all,
    With photographic arm.
Next day, they knew they must return,
    From old and back to new,
But later to projector turn,
    Their time in York review.
Along with all their folk at home,
    They'll go from new to old
And places where they once did roam,
    Will yet again behold.

Arnold Price

OLD TOM

Old Tom pulls his barrow on a warm afternoon,
Pipe in his mouth there is sweat on his brow
He rests for a while 'neath the shade of a tree
By the old village hall of Lazenby
Now he pulls out his matches with dirt stained hands
Then lights up his pipe all twisted and brown
And there he stands just drifting away,
Enjoying every minute of that summer day.

Now he pulls his barrow yes he pulls it behind,
Old Tom never rushes he just takes his time
Down the dirt track between the old sheds,
He stops, he gazes at the work ahead
With great thought and planning he looks on his acre
He has planted with carrots flowers and potato
He digs his plants with pride and with pain,
He works every day through sun and through rain.

Now at dusk he rests in an old wooden chair
And talks to himself there is no one else there
He pokes at the fire the flames dance and crack
Then mumbles to himself, when I was a lad
Then he spits in the embers and he draws on his pipe
And punches at the flies that dance in the night
Checking the time on his old pocket watch,
He moans to himself, the damn thing's stopped . . .

So he lifts himself gently from his old wooden chair
And breathes in deeply the soft evening air
He loads up his barrow with flowers and veg
Then wanders on home down by the Nags Head
Where he stops and he comments on the evening and the day
And talks of the seasons and their changing ways
Then he downs his glass bids good night all around
Never staggers out the door Old Tom is homeward bound

Karl Hague

THROSTLES NEST (ANOTHER NAME FOR BINGLEY)

Sad it is that my beloved Throstles Nest
bears witness to this satanic blemish,
bestirred by noisy, dusty traffic
passing through like lethal snake.

Plundering, thundering juggemauts
wending their uneasy way
bumper to sad bumper,
in the name of progress.

Station waiting-room
remembers roaring fire wintertime,
but now with urine-splattered walls
and repulsive graffiti,
this hive of degradation
has no place for decency.

Once, trains in smart uniform
sounded their friendly whistles passing by,
but now their diesel counterparts
hurry on unnoticed and unsung
lacking of character and personality.

Then trams trundled their shaky way
along their gleaming lines,
and children waved happily from aloft,
there was ample room to move,
and time for contemplation.

Where now? For if this is progress
the price to pay is high indeed.
But for all that
I shall seek my rest in Bingley,
for it is, and always will remain -
my Throstles Nest.

Winston White

52

BEAUTIFUL YORKSHIRE

Pretty villages, drystone walls
Curlews flying high
The county will inspire my soul
Until the day I die

The waterfalls, rivers, potholes
And the rocks
Sheepdogs working on the fells
Tending to their flocks

Church bells softly ringing
In the valley below
Sunsets in the evening
A breathtaking orange glow

The village pub, log fires,
Real ale and Sunday lunch
Hikers trudging down the lane
A red-faced happy bunch

Village fêtes and home-made jam
Cricket on the green
The beauty of the sky above
Cobalt and ultramarine

From The Cow and Calf to Ingleborough
Hills, valleys or desolate moor
A county with a beauty
That no man can ignore.

June Alethea Nichols

WAKEFIELD TOWN

Wakefield is a very big town,
Just a few miles from Leeds.
There's very good shops, in fact they're tops,
You don't have to go far for your needs.
Some Tuesdays, we visit all the charity shops,
They are shops Bez and I simply love,
When I talk to my friends I call them *Harrods*,
I think they've guessed my secret, by jove!
There's a lovely, big market three or four times a week,
To walk round is everyone's delight.
If you find any article hard to obtain
Just wait till Tuesday, you'll be alright.
We have a cathedral, majestic and tall;
A big prison where convicts do dwell;
There's a big police station, cafes and a town hall;
I've worked in one or two so I know them well.
There's Harrogate of course, with its soothing spa,
I wonder really, how many do get well?
I've never heard of anyone so far,
Speak of it as a magic spell.
In Wakefield there's a bingo hall called Gala,
With my friend, I attend every Saturday night,
I was quite lucky in 1993,
I'll win again if I play my cards right.
There are four or five churches I do recall,
Let's see, can I remember their titles?
There's St Catherine's, St Austin's and St Paul's,
English Martyrs, St John's and St Michael's.
So you see, this city, though small,
Has something for one and for all!

Ellen Hinnighan

THE MINOR PLEASURES OF HULL

Gently strolling round the Old Town
Deep shadows in the narrow, cobbled High Street
Warm red-brick buildings bearing
Ornate carvings of bounty, plenty,
Cornucopia, bearded Greek Gods
Pink and blue petunias nodding
In the cool Humber breeze
Behind their railings
Outside the severe
Maister House front
I step into the echoing courtyard of the Sailmaker's Arms
Through the cool carriage entrance
Sudden warmth and sunshine blazing
Hanging gardens of Babylon spring to mind
Yellow, red, profusion of colours
Dancing and bobbling down the courtyard walls
From dozens of hanging baskets
White pussycat tautly stalking
The caged parakeets chirping noisily
I am spellbound in delight
I smile
Breaking the spell I walk away
Soon I am breathing in the herb garden
Inhaling from the camomile lawn
Stark blue sky
Outlines the gravel works
Across the River Hull
Rusty barges chug sleepily
I am content.

J Pietrusiak

A TRIBUTE TO YORK

South born and bred we were posted to York
    Prepared to dislike the place
Resenting the move from family and friends
    Uncertain of what we must face!
We envisioned the north with dark mills and smoke
    With every pub called *The Black Bull*
The surprise we received when we viewed *Micklegate*
    made us feel we'd discovered a jewel!!
The Minster all floodlit; the old city walls;
    The daffodils blooming in spring
The quaint cobbled streets; the shambles and such
    The sight made our Southern hearts sing!
The small gabled shops and the *treasurer's house*
    Old churches that filled us with awe
Though we've travelled the world, we can honestly say,
    They impressed us as never before
The castle museum took us back through the ages
    The history of York was unfurled
And the famous old streets transported us back
    Into yesterday's wonderful world!
The people seemed friendly, warm-hearted indeed
    We felt we'd come in from the cold,
We bought a small house and made some new friends
    And York took us into its fold!
We've dwelt in this city for many good years
    And love every stick and old stone
We feel we belong; for having retired,
    York has become our true home.

Patricia Surman

A VIEW OF THE DALES

The Yorkshire Dales abound in spring
Lambs and buds and birds that sing
Wharfedale, Wensleydale, Nidderdale too
Sounds an alarm of the prospect in view.

The Wharfe flows quietly, the Nid serenely
The Ure through farms and fells it wends its way
The Swale in ever blooming pastures
Continues on from day to day.

Farmers sow and shepherds care
Grouse and pheasant adorn the air
Historical ruins, things of the past,
Abbeys and castles, all built to last.

With falls and fells and moors and glens,
Heaven sent pleasure for all God sends
Gauze and bracken the tints growing brighter
As the days grow longer and evenings lighter.

Time passes by and the calendar turns
Autumn arrives and glory returns
Be it sunshine or showers, beauty descends
In a spectrum of colour, as a rainbow ends.

The circle completes as winter draws in
There's fire in the grate at every dales' inn
As snow lays crisp and ponds freeze over
There is no better site between Orkney and Dover.

Edward Ramsey

IT'S A WONDERFUL PLACE . . .

It's a wonderful place is South Yorkshire.
And folk, they get on as they ought t'.
With no fuss and no flak
nor no posh yakkety-yak
life's for living and not looking back.

There's been stress and strain -
came like heavy rain,
on this lovely county of ours.
Came on me and you,
yet we saw it right through,
and with God's help we came bouncing back.

It's the future you see,
that affects you and me,
an' it's Him that's in charge of all that.
For he made this good place
part of his human race,
it's renewal He's longing to see.

That we thrive and we bloom,
just like bairns in the womb.
Our history great, there for us to take.
The castle and moorland and lakes,
a people so strong,
that others will long
to be with those who've got what it takes.

Ann Johnson

BINGLEY

Grinding along through Bingley
The endless traffic is hell
On the narrow A650
Where things are far from well.

They've argued about a bypass
For twenty years - and more
But can't agree where it should be
On the crowded valley floor.

Canal, road, river, railway
Each jostles for a place.
For the much needed bypass
There really isn't space.

Naught must sully Robert's Park,
Or change olde worlde Saltaire.
To desecrate the Bingley Bog
And its wildlife - who would dare?

Keep away from Beckfoot,
Off the grass in Myrtle Park,
The Druid's Altar is sacred
As is Lady Blantyre's Rock.

But there's another place for it,
Out of sight, and smell, and sound.
Expensive? It would be worth it -
A tunnel underground.

Mary Jackson

BROTHERTON

A mile north from Knottingley
lies this land of make-believe,
with curiosity people call,
a half of those don't leave!
Enchanted by its timeless air
or by the depth of mystery.
the village keeps a sacred hold
on its wealth of history.
Characters that come and go
whose names refuse to die,
Dodger Stretton, old Jack Wright!
Both legends in their time.
The River Aire at Ferrybridge
splits the north from west,
many battles here took place
to prove true north is best.
The tree-lined Coach Road -
deemed by most,
to be the place *they say*,
where Dick Turpin rode one night,
and almost lost his way.
Three coaching houses serve its folk
with choice of atmosphere,
but not matter where you choose to sup,
you travellers find us queer.
We've got the sights, we've got the views
and recently, we got gas,
yes, Brotherton is a village mate
which you don't want to pass.

Butch

EDGE OF THE MOORS

Oil-lamp lit the kitchen at night,
While candle glow gave bedroom light.
Hurricane lamp for stable and byre.
Peat was smouldering on open fire.
Thick, homecured rashers of ham
Sizzling in black, hooked frying-pan.
On that farm seventy years ago.

Treasured sampler on parlour wall,
Grandfather clock standing in hall.
Framed text above the mantelpiece,
Family photos on sideboard piece,
Feather mattress on brass-knobbed bed,
Home-made patchwork quilted bedspread.
Seventy years ago.

Sides of bacon in dairy hooked.
Bread and pies in side-oven cooked.
Eggs and butter ready to sell.
Drinking water drawn from well.
Round haystacks children chased by day,
Ludo and Snap were night-time play.
Seventy years ago.

Walking was the transport mode,
Children to school did trudge by road.
While cycling was a faster way,
Horse and trap conveyed on market day.
Sandy roads were oft deep-rutted,
Many a bridge was wooden slatted.
Seventy years ago.

Florence Needler

NOSTALGIC MEMORIES (GRAN'S)

In days of yore when houses stood in rows
and vogue was Grandma's iron mangle,
what 'ere the weather be it rain or snow
washday on rota saved a wrangle.
Wash-house set pot to boiling was got,
as deftly clothes were sorted on flagstone floor.
Gran scrubbed, possed, rubbed, the outside world she quite forgot
while boiling water with piggin kept hung behind the door.
The heavy rollers of mangle applying compression,
expressing water to send it gushing
from shirts, collars and garments we cannot mention
to save Grandma's face from blushing.
When clog irons on cobbles we heard clatter
by people who long hours worked in the mill.
When pawnbroker was poor man's banker
then steps were ruddled and fine line drawn on windowsill.
Homelife was simple, and dialect broad-spoken,
memory stirs still of the aroma of new baked bread,
of blackleaded range from whose oven teacakes were taken
to spread thick with butter, we did not calories dread.
On golden days the countryside was the garden's extension
to roam at will o'er wood, vale and hill,
seasons each holding its own beauty beyond mention,
imagination ne'er lacking the long days with ease we did fill.
Billberry, blackberry, elderberry each in their season we gathered
oblivious of stains or clothes on thorns being torn.
All is forgiven when fruit in jam-pan with sugar was smothered
as at day's end pictures in fire we created while
hugging cocoa mugs, then bed in pyjamas of flannelette warm.

M M Walker

BINGLEY UPON AIRE

Once Bingley awoke to the early call of blackbird and robin,
And the river Aire ran bright and clean,
Rippling and gurgling in the early dawn air,
Weaving its happy and winding way,
To greet the dawn of another working day.
Almond and cherry along Main Street bloomed,
Their pink, orange blossom drifting in the breeze.
Shop upon shop displaying their gaudy merchandise,
Their every ware made by hand, forgotten, unknown.
Then came the telltale clank of tramcar meandering,
From Crossflatts thro' to Bradford, then back again,
See boats on the river plying for pleasure,
And barges trafficking coal for furnace,
Along the dark waters of the Leeds-Liverpool canal.
Then down to Myrtle Park to greet one and all,
To spend many an hour in the sun,
Kids running wild, bronzed and contented,
While come evening teenagers to the Prinny went dancing,
Or to Myrtle and Hipperdrome held their delight,
Films that thrilled you night after night.
Workers streamed to mills, their service to give,
Spinning and twisting in order to live.
On calm, summer's evenings long gone by,
The parish church bells called for prayer.
Once more into darkness night would fall,
While stars above Altar Rock twinkled wide-eyed,
This was the Aire Valley, the Bingley we loved.
These are the memories we must treasure forever.
Long gone now, forgotten, betrayed.
With plans for a bypass. A new Bingley outlaid.

R Whitehead

UNTITLED

West Yorkshire is the place to be
That's if you like their honesty
For they will tell you what they think
No matter if it includes you in.
While searching for an answer
And turning strawberry pink
They're wondering why you're looking like this
Has your skin gone suddenly thin?
While taking in their blank dismay
You realise they are made this way
They're not trying to make you look small
Only to keep you on the ball.
At last you recognise true worth
It's been inherited from birth
And when you're feeling ill and down
Their caring knows no bounds.
Your brow becomes theirs to mop
Then off they go to shop
They come back with a survival kit
Needed to pull you through
It's their one aim to see you fit
And this they're going to do.
You're grateful for this take-over plan
What good is a dying swan?
Your energy is at such a low ebb
As it escapes through your throbbing head
With relief you sink into bed
But luck has sent you a mother-hen
Until you're on your feet again.
The sands of time holds the key to understanding
While true grit helps to unify the binding.
What better mixture can you have
To cement a lasting friendship path?

A Mitchell

FOOTBALL SUPPORTER

Well I would be a
Football supporter
And there I was plain
As could be
Two jumpers, three trousers,
Two headscarves
I can't stand
The cold you see
That Sunday morning
Mexborough District
Were giving it their all
But instead of a goal
The striker,
Accidentally stuck one
On me!
And I was felled
Like a Blaster-Bates chimney
I just felt as daft
As a brush
All these good-looking blokes
All round me
Waiting to sponge me mush
Now I know what it feels like
To get zonked on the head
By the ball
So I said,
'Now I'm fully recovered,'
And standing on me two feet
Well, I'll keep eyes front
In future
So I can make
A faster retreat.

Audrey Gamble

DONCASTER MARKET

You board the bus, with your Pensioner's Pass,
(And, reader, the word is pronounced like *lass*,
For Yorkshire speech is special, you see -
Not like announcers on t' BBC!)

As you travel along, you look at the view,
Then talk to the lady who's next to you;
Yorkshire folk are fond of a chat,
And helpful to strangers - no doubt about that.

Your neighbour tells you it's market day,
You get off the bus and she shows you the way.
You visit the market, and there you find
Wonderful stalls of every kind!

What a display! From bangles and beads,
To the fruit and veg that the family needs;
From the crusty bread (how nice it looks!)
To the toys and games, the comics and books;

From the jumpers and socks, the slippers and shoes,
To the pots and pans, and things that we use
In the kitchen. And then, there's fabulous fish,
As cheap and as fresh as you ever could wish!

And the way those stallholders cry their wares -
No wonder the newcomer stands and stares
And listens, enthralled, to the local sound:
'Lovely bananas - thirty a pound!'

All too soon, it's closing time;
And here's the end of this little rhyme.
But let me assure you, before I go:
Doncaster Market's the *best* one I know!

June Tomlinson

RYEDALE

There are places of outstanding beauty I know
Places I in my lifetime , alas cannot go
But those I have seen can never compare
With the rugged and wonderful Yorkshire we share

Come and visit our coast, at its villages stay
Places like Staithes, or Robin-Hoods-Bay
There's a timeless beauty in sunshine or rain
You'll want to return again and again.

And parts of Yorkshire can vary so much
Industry, farming, mining, and such
But my part of Yorkshire is Ryedale, and cast
In moulds of beauty and peace unsurpassed.

Take a walk up the dales in summer or spring
Such a wealth of flowers to make your heart sing.
and though the wild moor may seem bleak and cold
When the heather's in bloom it's a sight to behold.

Our historic houses are worthy of viewing
Each abbey too, though classed as a ruin
In the old market towns find a bargain or so
Try the bar meals, they really are something you know.

But for all the beauty that Ryedale can boast
That isn't the thing that I'd brag about most.
It's the people that make life really worthwhile
Their wit and humour cause many a smile.

Oh! They do seem to know a good deal when it's made
And they always call a spade a spade
But kindly, and helpful and welcoming they
So Ryedale in Yorkshire is where I shall stay.

Eva Ward

THE RETURN

High, rusty hangars long deserted
Control tower open to the sky
Nissen huts high bramble skirted
Under wheat the runways lie.

Silent dispersals under thick hawthorns
And aged rooks in ancient trees
Remembering when the misty dawns
Vibrated with Merlin and Hercules.

The caravan only in fancy seen
Long shadowed in the fading light
Where we waited for the green
To send us off into the night.

Nearby farm with pantiles red
Where the kettle was always on
And where they would lie abed
Counting us in, one by one.

Grey Norman church among the trees
Where airman and crusader rest
A Wesley hymn caught on the breeze
The gathered host in Sunday best.

They praise the good Lord in heaven
From sturdy earthbound pews
And tend the rows of seven by seven
White headstones of the bomber crews.

Ronald Gatenby

INHERITANCE

There is a place on English soil
A rarer breed is found
Where its people, were they for sale
Would cost a higher pound.

Reward is gained through honest toil
And not urged on by greed,
Within the realm of the white rose
The wisest take their lead
Children are taught from early years
What strangers fail to learn,
That here, they're judged by what they do
And not how much they earn.

You is Tha' and right is ray't,
We wear boo'its upon our feet,
The money in our purse is *dough*
And stars are seen at 'neet.

The kettle's put straight on t' boil
When strangers come to tea
No matter, the colour of your skin
Of from which creed you be.
Like our now abandoned seams of coal
Pride's embedded deep, so that
Neither the farmer's plough
Nor miner's roughened hands can reap.

You may find the fiscal head
In some more southern part
But 'tis to England's largest county
That she entrusts her heart.

Denise Stables

SLEEPING PAVEMENTS

I stare at the cold, silent pavements, thinking not much time
has passed, since they echoed to sounds so different as now.
I think of the mantle of happy humanity, not so long ago adorning
them.
Children brandishing ice cream cornets, some in a manner not unlike
edible Olympic torches, some gleeful owners waving them
recklessly,
to give the pavements a share of the tasty contents, like seagull
droppings. A nearby lucky dogs lick, a dog must be quick with
tongue,
before ice cream is sandwiched between shoe sole and pavement.

As day merges with night and litter bins overflow, discarded
empty crisp packets, fish and chip papers, endless other droppings
discarded by a carefree canopy of people, gave the pavements their
summertime confetti. All seemed happy confusion, I do not think
the pavements minded, they must have felt in tune, with the carefree
mood of their human canopy.

Now they are cold, untrod in such a manner, all the revellers
have left for inland comfort. The pavements must remain to echo
the few lonely treads. Autumn leaves tried to comfort, offering
nature's leafy confetti, but were not allowed to remain for long.
Soon to be gathered' to make scented smoke, some were gather'd
by a wind gaining winter strength, scattering them on new ground
some landing in strange hiding places.

These places must slumber uneasy, through the winter often
suffering the cold, wind-driven salty spray covering, thrown by
an unfriendly noisy north seas neighbour. When winter approaches
it's seasonal end, faint sunlight will warm these pavements,
to prepare them once again to play their seasonal role.

L B Vickers

BELATED PROTEST

Born and bred in Bradford's fair town
With its solid stone centre until some
Schizophrenic architects pulled it down.
Them that did it did not go unopposed:
There were thousands signed petitions
From all walks of life but they just
Went ahead and had it bulldozed.
Hitler couldn't have done a better
Job with a bomb.
Beautiful buildings were destroyed:
God knows where their crazy ideas
Came from.
What they did to Bradford was criminal:
The likes of the Swann Arcade and the
Mechanics Institute could have been
Restored with the cost minimal.
To see what emerged from all the rubble
Was nothing more than a concrete shanty
Town which has caused nothing but trouble.
They wanted to give Bradford a modern look
But the schizophrenic architects must have
Used a blueprint from a cheap DIY book.
Every time I go into Bradford my heart bleeds
Because less than ten miles away I can see that
They are carefully restoring the centre of Leeds.
Born and bred in Bradford's fair town
With its solid stone centre until some
Schizophrenic architects pulled it down.

Alan Holdsworth

SEMER WATER

That evening
when we pulled the boats ashore
the air drifted into stillness
so still a dog yapped once for us in Stalling Busk or Marsett
and martins dabbed their quick, black wings
in the sun's steaming blood-cauldron.

After the clatter of our eating
a peace descended
unhumanly on the far fells
- and its immensity demanded worship:
fear of the dark, perhaps:
but caves are caves, in limestone or the soul,
or in the paddle-calloused hand that holds the match
that lights the driftwood fire.

We crouched and blew and coughed
and still the birds called goodnight behind our senses
in the pathless meadows and looming hills.
But the fire blazed. Hallelujah!
Twelve pumpkin faces and it's Hallowe'en.

Worship: the soft spell of driftwood incense
woven with Semer Water's dank, dark sweat
and a million small dreaming flowers on the fells;
the hill-farm's cow-breath, choirstall whispers from invisible trees,
- we don't touch, we don't care, we're tough, we're Adventure School,
outward-bound, inward-bound . . .

John Avison

LINES WRITTEN IN A COUNTRY VILLAGE

'Life in West Yorkshire! By it's grand to be here!'
Said Albert the blacksmith as he downed his brown beer:
I live in a village with all of my mates,
The living is cheap, and so are the rates,
We grow our own cabbage, we grow our own spuds,
Our hens lay aplenty: our cows chew their cuds,
Our neighbours are honest, they're straight down the line,
A spade is a spade, well most of the time!
We all have allotments, and tell a good yarn,
And we always switch on for that Emmerdale Farm,
We never watch Neighbours, or Home and Away,
We'd rather play bowls or go out for the day,
The vicar's right welcome, though he never stays long,
He's always so busy putting right what is wrong.
We sit through his sermons, and never nod off,
We can't anyway, the curate's a cough.
We sing all the hymns with gusto and soul:
And pray that we never get put on the dole:
The annual outing to Scarborough or Brid.
Takes place in July, and we always take Sid,
For Sid is our mascot, he's our village goat,
And besides he likes sailing in a Peaseholme Park boat!
We drink in our local, The Old Dog and Gun,
We meet in the Tap Room and have lots of fun,
We've a domino-dart league, and pea and pie treats,
Our homes are all tidy, and so are the streets,
You can keep your big towns and your sprawling suburbs
Our West Yorkshire village, well we think its superb!
'What's the name of this place? 'Can't tell you my son,
If I told you that, you'd all want to come!'

Rod Coope

YORKY'S LAMENT

I've lived and loved in tropic climes,
but still an' all, I find,
rain washed skies
and cool blue eyes
keep walking into my mind.

For late at night as I lay awake
to a mad mosquito's whine,
I seem to see
where I need to be -
on those Pennine Hills of mine.

When winter strides across the moor.
When the moon sheds a misty light.
And the village green
lies crisp and clean
after snow falls in the night.

When flowers bloom in Bronteland,
apple blossom in the trees.
A perfume born
on an April morn,
then lost on a wayward breeze.

Picnics in a summer field.
The girl with the golden hair.
The laugh I'd hear
so sweet and clear.
Like the stream that's bubblin' there.

The sun, the sea, the islands.
A kiss by a blue lagoon.
I'd swap all those
for a Yorkshire rose
on a rainy afternoon.

Colin Moore

A THOUGHT FOR YORKSHIRE

Get yourself comfy take a seat,
this journey is easy on the feet.
Close your eyes, I'll show you a place,
full of character, pose and grace.
The interest of this trip you'll not tire,
we are on our way to Yorkshire.
Interesting knowledge can be found,
in every town you look around.
There's York with its regal Minster,
tall, aloof, and grand that's her.
Sheffield has its famous steel foundries,
oversea exports, limitless boundries.
Doncaster plant attributed lots,
by making the Mallard and flying Scott's.
On the track you'll rarely see um,
but will if you go to the railway museum.
On other things there's praise to sing,
what about the great Yorkshire pudding.
When the weather's nice don't stay indoors,
take a hike round the dales or moors.
Lucious green fields, quite serene,
beautiful landscapes, what never been?
Even at sport we take a pat on the back,
Sheffield Wednesday and United, Freddie Trueman, Geoff Boycott
                                          and people like that.

One thing I just can't leave out,
Is the lingo, has tha got, I an't go nowt.
Yorkshire people are full of fun,
with there nay lad tha can't do that and eeh by gum.
So if my words have stirred the way you feel,
come and see this great place for real.

Janet Davison

THE RENTMAN

Get under the window
And don't be seen
The rentman is coming
And we haven't a bean

Don't make a sound
His ears are like wings
I'll give you a clout
If he hears anything

Don't even breathe
And close your eyes
Lay down flat
Till I tell you to rise

When you hear his hobnails
Go round to the rear
Get to the window
And see if all's clear
Then you're a good boy
My little dear.

Alien Tortice

DESTINATION

The 9.40 for Manchester, calling at New Pudsey, Bradford,
Halifax, Sowerby Bridge, Hebden Bridge, Todmorden . . .

By accident one day I caught that train
(Bad-tempered, bus missed, and in a hurry).
Till Halifax I noticed only rain,
Acting out its own persistent fury.
As we pulled out, though, one sharp shaft of sun
Stuck silver from wet grass. Black walls now gleamed.
I found myself intrigued as if I'd come
On some lost landscape. Was it as it seemed?

In Hebden houses zigzagged up the hill
Like vertigo made real - bewildering.
By now the sky was blue, the air quite still
And, in the valley, first buds opening.
I met you - late remember - and surprised
You with my wonder. Months passed but when,
Taking, by chance, that route, you realised,
We knew we were at home here, now as then.

Theresa Sowerby

FROM THE EAST TO THE NORTH

I am earthbound now.
No longer hearing
Foghorns moaning on the Humber,
Muffled sound in the dawn,
Seagulls screaming their freedom
Harsh beauty in their cries.

I am earthbound now.
No longer seeing
Sand dunes where once I played
They are flattened, dissolved away,
But waves still crash, metallic and cold,
Against crumbling sea walls.

I am earthbound now.
The gulls I see follow tractors.
No light on water here
No smell of salt or fish.
A strange beauty,
Tamed, ploughed, contained.

My home is earthbound now
But my soul still flows to the sea.

Catherine Mitchell

LANDSCAPE IN A QUARRY

Landscape - bare, spare desolate
Soil thin and sterile
Tufts of coarse grass, hardy plants
Struggle to survive and keep alive
Alongside small boulders
Dandelions, ragwort, splashes of gold
Enhance, among this grey expanse.
Stretching on two sides - a mighty bluff
Barred, banded and scarred with red and yellow
A cunningly devised snare; a place of peril.
At one end a cluster of trees
The breeze stirs and rustles the wrestling boughs
Deep tangled undergrowth forms in their shade
A wondrous glade
A real delight found in this wildemess so stark.
Adjacent to the quarry is a rough, cinder path
Leading to a steep incline
To plod up the traveller must
Half-choked in swirling clouds of dust
Flanked on either side, hawthorn bushes rough
their branches tough, jut out forbiddingly,
Stubborn bindweed, nettles and discoloured grass
All abound in the hedgerows as you pass
nearby elderberry trees flourish
In a lacework of delicate white meadowsweet
On their long weak stems goosegrass grows
Rose bay willow herb also blows,
This primeval wilderness, a portion of open hell
With its ragged beauty ought to be preserved forever.

Pauline Fletcher

MY YORKSHIRE

I have no wish to visit lands
Be them near or far
I have no wish to travel the world
In an aeroplane, ship or a car

I do not long for a tropical isle
Where palm trees on golden sands grow
Or visit the lands where mountains are climbed
With their tall peaks covered in snow

For I love this land where swallows fly
And where the summer follows the spring
To walk over the moors or down country lanes
Where birds in the hedges do sing

So give me this land where people are free
Where my father before me did roam
For this is my land the place I was born
My Yorkshire, my county, my home.

Colin Garner

NORTH YORKSHIRE

What does North Yorkshire mean?
Lambs and daffodils and running stream.
The Wolds, the Moors, seasons come and go.
Summer breezes or winter snow.
Time stands still on a *balmy* day
Watching the farmers reaping the hay.
A walk thro' the woods in a shower of rain
Look out for the swallows as they return again.
A trip to the bay as evening falls
and listen to the gulls as each one calls.

These things mean a lot to a North Yorkshire Tyke.
Well that's all for now, I'm off on me bike!

Mary H Wood

FAMILY OUTING

English cherry blossom, curtseying brides,
Graceful ghosts from a vanquished kingdom,
Dancing among the wakening greens of the woodland.

Winter magic, tossing whiteness,
Snowy softness, billowing froth,
Festival virgin, impudent glory,
Gracing the warmer world.

Gentle invader, tiptoeing trespasser,
Restless intruder among the fronds and the foliage.

Desolate day of battering words,
Condemned cell of a relationship,
Slammed doors, final exits;
Yet raised to grace by that dancing lightness,
Whiteness, magical souvenir
Of beauty that wins over pain.
Silver scars wake no tragic echoes,
Only the dance and the lightness remain.

Ruth P Singer

THE GHOST OF ACASTER AIRFIELD

Developers arrived one day, and surveyed a piece of land.
'We'll build 5,000 houses here - now wouldn't that be grand?'
And the ghost of Acaster Airfield stirred uneasily.

But the splendid folk of Acaster, not liking what they heard.
Decided to retaliate; began their loins to gird.
But the ghost of Acaster Airfield was nervous.

The planners planned, and then unplanned; the green belt was in
                                                            doubt,
But the people were determined to keep the builders out.
And the ghost of Acaster Airfield began to hope.

They formed a strong committee, which took the name of *Poach*.
And fought off all the planners, and dared them to encroach.
And the ghost of Acaster Airfield lay low.

Then the powers-that-be decided: 'The land is in green belt.'
So the goodly folk of Acaster, down in thanksgiving knelt.
Now the ghost of Acaster Airfield walks free.

Genevieve Grewer

YORK MINSTER

It reigns in majesty over us,
Aeons have passed since its blessing.
Through all the city's changing fortunes
It has rested in solitary splendour.

A mountain of stone - poetically designed
Overlooking the town in grandeur.
Witnessing the tourists, the razz-a-ma-tazz,
Hotels, bed and breakfast, boutiques.

Undismayed by today's feckless crowd,
Its beauty is offered to all.
For was it not always like this,
All manner of folk coming to gawp?

Pilgrims were medieval tourists.
Holy pilgrimage? For some. Not all.
An outing, a rattling, good party,
Excitement - something different to do.

Who will visit and look in the future?
Universe travellers from way out in space?
Will they stare at our Minster in wonder
And silently offer a prayer?

Joan Clark

THE COUNTRYSIDE

Early morning dew settles on newly nurtured grass.
Crisp beneath my feet, stepping out on a walk into heaven.
Yorkshire countryside is in a different class.
The pride in your heart, tells you as you ramble through the heather.
Take deep breaths, finding it hard to take it in
Stop and look around, clear your mind of all thoughts of the city.
The hustle and bustle, the rush hour traffic and the din.
They'll never realise how beautiful this is for those I pity.
Gaze over the hillside, and a landscape and sigh
No buildings, no cranes, no cars, busses or noise
Only Mother Nature's greatest work of art passes by
And the only sound is your own voice
How can they rape it? And tear it apart?
Putting up Power Stations, and Nuclear bases
A country so strong in a Yorkshire man's heart
You ought to bow your heads, and hide your faces.

Mark Evans

YORKSHIRE

A name that conjures up so many different sights,
From steel mills to busy roads, green fields and seaside lights.
Proud people, hard working miners seeking jobs to use their skills,
There are forests, lakes, farms and snow-capped hills,
Beauty surrounded by rough hedges and neat stone walls,
Magnificent York Minster and its hallowed halls,
Cottage gardens and stately homes abound -
Visit Scarborough's unique *Theatre in the Round*
The heather clad moors, the Wolds and Dales
Brings a special delight that never fails.
Hear those melodious village bands - the Silver and the Brass,
I'm so happy to have been *raised a Yorkshire lass!*

Sheila Stead

WESTERLY HERITAGE

I wor niver fat, nor ower thin
But ow I luvved mi Sunday din.
Piles o' tatties, cabbage too
If we got lucky, rabbit stew.
Mi' eyes allus stuck ont' oven's ledge
Waitin' fer that golden wedge
Ma said, 'Nowt to beat pudden, mi bonny lass'
Dad giv' it a nod an filled up er glass.
Then on wi' mi coit afore it got dark
And off fer a run to bowlin' park
Prancing int' sunshine, even in rains
Dodgin' t'signal man, watchin' fer trains
Then thru' park gates, kids laking int' pond
But I liked to stare at wot wer beyond.
Fields like tablecloths, trees lent green lace
Daisies wor dropt pearls, buttercups hed place,
Far, far away yon heather, amethyst true
And orl abart mi clogs, dandelions blew.
A h've getten owd tha knaws, needin' mi fire
But cud niver forget ah realm, comely Yorkshire.

F Sexton

THE YORKSHIRE SHOW

It's great living in the land of the Yorkshire pud
Yorkshire ham, pork pies, the dales and sun
You never have to travel far to find some fun,
Dark mills, deep mines, chocolate making, what's your line,
People proud mixing well, living together fine.
Land of rugby, football, cricket all.
Where people can walk tall,
A land with a past, full of grace
A land as big as its heart filled with people of every race,
No matter where you go it's just one big Yorkshire show.

John David Bone

HILL SPELL

Up, where hill meets sky
And curlews cry,
There, washed walls climb steep
And mist-clouds weep

Look! Clear water flows
But quickly goes
Down, through caverns deep,
Where sea-beds sleep.

Once, a green-eyed lad
Came, wond'ring, glad.
Straight, a bond was made -
Stays un-decayed.

Again, my need is strong,
I must along,
Seek some fresh release
In precious peace.

Neville Slack

ROCHE ABBEY

R uins of a former limestone, Gothic glory, St Mary's,
O pen to the public gaze
C an be glimpsed from the slope above the verdant valley
H eavenly on a mild summer's
E vening when an
A rena for performing arts with
B asking picnickers below the transept
B oasting candelabra on starched white cloths
E vocations of the spirits of former days - Capability Brown and
Y esteryear's Cistercians celebrating the mysteries of the cross.

C G Crehan

WUTHERING HEIGHTS

I'm a Haworth lass, born and bred,
These moorland paths I often tread,
Here, the moor in all its glory
Reminds me of that Brontë story:
Of Heathcliff and Cathy
And their turbulent love -
Wild as the moors with stormy skies above.
The rain clouds gather as we trudge through the heather
Beside a moorland track,
As we approach the house we startle the grouse
And their call says 'Go back, go back.'
We pass a stream, now the going is tough,
Soon we reach Top Withens and the weather is rough.
We stay awhile to drink in the scenery
And gaze at the rushes, the sheep and the greenery.
We retrace our steps as daylight ends
On the downward path which winds and bends
Back, towards Gimmerton until we return once more
To Wuthering Heights, high on Haworth Moor.

Dorothy Nixon

YORKSHIRE

Of all the many counties Yorkshire stands supreme
Full many a year I've lived here and watched the changing scene
Yorkshire has great cities but Leeds outshines the rest
The floral parks, its many shops are of the very best
Travel from the heart of Leeds by train or bus or car
To visit well-known places, some near and some afar
The Yorkshire Dales and, of course, the rugged Ilkley Moor
Their scenery and grandeur we really do adore
I've stood in many airports and travelled far and wide
But Yorkshire is where I'm happiest and always will abide.

Elsa Rhodes

DENHOLME - A YORKSHIRE VILLAGE

There was a pride in my village
Once, long ago, when folk with clog shod feet, would go,
Five abreast down to the mill,
To the hooters sound, I hear it still,
Our park and bandstand owe their birth,
To the shuttle and loom,
And the workers' worth,
Weavers' houses built to last,
Tell tales of success from our village past,
Mansions were built to show to all,
The wealth of this Pennine village small,
Now time and progress have left their mark,
The bandstand is crumbling in the park,
Graffiti defaces each empty space
There is no pride now in this place
Does no-one notice? Does no-one care?
The mill closed down splintered windows stare,
The once grand clock, our village pride,
Has lost its face on every side,
My Yorkshire in 1994 is sad,
Bewildered, lost and poor.

Kate Heaton

CHANGES AT HEPTONSTALL

Standing on its grit stone height
Overlooking three main valleys,
Many changes this village has seen.
Saxon and Norman have trodden its alleys.
Under the tarmac the sets are still there,
And maybe below them the cobbles are found,
Between which the grass grew in days of the plague.

Centre of all is the church of St Thomas,
Gazing down from its gothic grandeur
On what remains of its gale-ruined ancestor.
Scanning too a graveyard so ancient
That many are lost who were first laid to rest.
No room herein for the moderns to lie,
They find their rest in the new yard nearby.

Battered and gale-tossed throughout the ages
The grit of survival withstands all the rages;
And Royalist and Roundhead and Royalist again
Captured this castle of grit on the hill.
Each in their turn would ring the changes,
Calling for loyalty, each to their cause:
But rigid and durable the grit at the core.

Then later on, a different loyalty
As Wesley rode the crowded streets.
Did they conform, these men on the hill,
Or did they succumb to the fiery preacher?
Though these decisions are now in the past
No doubt surrounds the present feature,
The graveyard is full at the eight-sided chapel.

Characters come and characters go
And many have passed through this village of grit,
Their lives and legends are landmarks historic.
Now gone are those worthies and gone is the heart
Of this old, weathered village here on the height.
What different changes St Thomas is ringing
To a modern community here on the hill.

John Brandon

YORKSHIRE SPIRIT

This is the heart of the industrial world,
Where everything began;
Scarred by the search sewn into our past,
The place where the first race ran.
Cobbled streets and silent mills,
Echoes of yesterday's crimes,
Intermingled with modern shopping arcades,
Showing the sign of the times.
But the hills stand steady,
Unmoving, unchanged,
Watching the perpetual turmoil;
Quiet and green with sparkling streams,
Like a friend at their most loyal.
This is a place of inspiration and dreams,
Gained within these valleys and hills;
A place rich in diversity and character,
Pleasurable without unwanted frills.

Stuart J Firth (16)

YORKSHIRE SNIPPETS

Walk
In York.
History lives.
Everything gives
Visitors part
Of Yorkshire's heart.

Yorkshire Dales,
Yorkshire Ales,
Healthy walks,
Friendly talks.
All give pleasure
In good measure.

Molly Smithson

ME ROOTS

I used to live in Yorkshire, I'm Yorkshire born and bred,
but now I've moved far away and live in France instead.

I remember Dale Road tramsheds and trolley buses too,
the Whitehall *caff* in Rotherham and Speed's as well - do you?

I remember folks said thee and tha and sithee lad look 'ere -
something's are changing all the time but the dialect no fear!

I remember *Sunshine Corner* and Whitsuntide parades,
the statues fair with roundabouts and ha'penny arcades.

I used to live in Yorkshire and though I'm far away
from time to time I make a trip and love to hear folks say -

'Nice to see yer! Ah tha doin?' 'What's them *Frenchies* like?' -
is it true they wear striped vests and always ride a bike?

The muck, the grime I miss it all and 'specially Yorkshire pudden -
Parkin, tripe and apple pie - me mother made a good un!

I used to live in Yorkshire, I'm Yorkshire through and through
but though I've moved so far away my heart is still with you.

Josie Brown

UNTITLED

Y orkshire, oh Yorkshire we all declare
O f all the counties, none are more fair.
R olling moors from Whitby, Goathland and Sleights
K eeping us happy with many highlights,
S unshine or showers we really don't mind,
H amlets at the end of roads that wind.
I n town or village your heart will soar
R idings three are there to explore
E very part of the dales and the moor.

Audrey Loxton

WEST YORKSHIRE MUCK

Pleasant vibes exude warmly from
everywhere; dark streets, light
alleys, verdant moisture dripping
from housetops, the postman bright
greets all with a winning smile
glittering on his bicycle, the corner shop
opening for early day, busy already
with Mrs This and That, a humming drop
in a tireless ocean of labyrinths,
of byways opening out or shutting in,
ginnels and snickets avoiding the
teeming Saturday rush, a silenced din
blending with West Yorkshire muck
and stained brass, dishevelled children
muscling in on a lost copper coin
making a melee of laughter their den.

Gail Mary Leadley

WHERE THERE'S MUCK

We want the best, we tend to say,
Let's live for tomorrow, not just today,
We northerners *know* the price that's to pay
With coal mines, and pit heaps in view every day.
At the bottom of our gardens
we've power-stations spewing,
If they were down south, the environment
                                        they'd ruin.
We are now used, to the rape of our county,
To allow us the thought of dreaming of bounty
As things are going, there will soon
                              be not pits
And now with clean air, we may reap
                              some benefits.

J Addison

YORKSHIRE

Conveniently placed between North and South
Stretching way out to the coast.
Mile upon mile of countryside this County of
Yorkshire can boast.

Historical cities, Museums in towns, there's
lots for us all to explore. We can don on
our boots, hike up the hills, walk on the vast
open moor.

Picturesque villages, magnificent views all
within easy reach of our towns, Potholes,
Caverns, Ancient stones, natural beauty abounds.

Fresh air and open spaces at no cost for us all
to share, for there's plenty of it up in Yorkshire
for this I do declare.

Maureen Beaumont

HOME OF MINE

Ageing buildings and wondrous dales,
Green-clad hills rambling vales,
with wheatfields that nod and rivers that flow,
where cattle are grazing in pastures below
with towns and gardens, cliffs and rocks,
ministers and churches with very old clocks.
The charming woodland in all its greenery,
the wolds stretch for miles in all the scenery.
The moorland solitude is something rare
with heather almost everywhere.
People surrounded by ecstasy -
with all these wonders this must be,
the end of my anthology.

Barbara Ward

THE WHINMOOR WAY

Pencil in every Friday
Same time, same bus, same pub.
Fellas with tailored trousers, Italian shirts
Lasses look like a glamorous gaze.
See the multipockets of people chat,
Can't wait to get down clubbin',
The latest dance moves my fave,
Changing quicker than the Hot Shot Top 10.
Lads guzzle bottled beer with lime, no glass - thanks.
It's cocktail concoctions for the girls,
No Guinness served here.
Let's go place to place, see some get hitched,
Others stick together, the usual gang.
Many work together, talk of the dreaded place.
We wanna forget work, it's Friday.
Let's get *blindo,* get a cab, get home.
First a kebab. Calories? They don't count.
The old folks house, our hotel, best not wake 'em.
Sleep it off Saturday, ready for the next session.
Money and sense? Nightlife always rules the day.

Mark Allinson

SPIRIT OF LIFE

Spirit of life, guide me through,
let me envisage the life I once knew.
Words are spoken, thoughts are silent,
the mind is so complex,
I don't understand what it's saying to me.

What does it want me to be?
Still trying to analyse its values
Wondering, will I see the way clear?
suddenly a light is near.

A ray of hope, the sun's beam shines through.

'Search for your soul, go deep within,
meditate with your mind and body.

Ask yourself, what do I want from life?
and don't return to the past.

Go forward, your path is clear,
the Spirit of Life will always be here.'

Jarusi Warburton

THIS YORKSHIRE MOOR

At dawn the moors roll soft and grey,
And drifting mists veil valley floors,
Each grass-blade bears a shining bead of glass,
And early sunlight knocks on farmhouse doors.
Birdsong celebrates the promise of the day,
As if each knows the cat has curled to sleep,
And with his dog and crook the shepherd climbs
The heathered hills to huddled sheep.
He walks pannier tracks that monks once trod,
By velvet springs and weathered walls,
And as the day moves ever on,
The sun sleeps low and the red deer calls.
Now home is close, down in the dale,
With promise of warmth and a welcome chair,
A sky so black cloaks house and hill,
And a thousand stars pierce frosty air.
'Tis bitter cold,' the farmer grumbles,
As the tabby cat climbs on his knee,
But he would not swap this Yorkshire moor,
So tumbled, wild, and fierce, and free.

Mandy Huggins

YORKSHIRE WAY

Many people think that Yorkshire's full of coal mines and mills
But we've got parks and gardens and lovely rolling hills
For friendliness we are renowned
And our generosity knows no bounds.

Why don't you pay a visit to see for yourself?
For we have a lot of things more precious than wealth
There's the cascading waters of lovely *Aysgarth Falls*
Also there's the majesty of *Burton Agnes Hall*.

There's a parsonage at *Harworth* home of the *Bronte* clan
And then of course there's *Whitby* where the myth of *Dracula* began
We've racecourses stately homes and leisure parks as well
And the lovely *Fountains Abbey* on the banks of the *River Skell*.

So if you fancy a trip out one day
Why don't you come down *Yorkshire Way?*

Mary Powell

APPROACHING HELMSLEY - EVENING

I do not come on softly-sandalled feet
Looking towards your castellated keep.
Nor do I reign my horse and, pausing still,
Watch as the evening haze creeps down the hill,
Closing the doors of houses to the night,
Narrowing windows to a candlelight.

I come with echoing engine's humming speed,
Proofed, in a box on wheels, against the need
To think on the lifeblood of this little place,
Ponder the night dreams of so small a space.
Only the wanderer, open to the skies,
Captures the essence where he lives and dies.

Elizabeth Lester

THOUGHTS OF YORKSHIRE

Wondrous moors stretch out before me
Reaching far beyond my sight
Richly draped with purple heather
Ablaze beneath the golden light.
Harmonious with the blue horizon
Rocky mounds blend so divine
I drift bewitched by all this beauty
O'er this sunkissed land so fine.
Blessed am I to see this beauty
Spread before mine humble eyes
Awakening in my heart a yearning
That this splendour never dies.

Angela Melvin

END OF AN ERA

We used to warm
the nation
We produced coal
with pride
But they're closing down
our industry
The need for our skills
has died

So we will adapt
change our ways
Watch our heritage
slip by
But we're not saying
it'll be easy
And we will always
question why.

Ian Mylchreest

SONNET TO SPRING

Snowdrops then crocus heralding the spring,
Season of hopefulness after the gloom.
Hedgehogs awakening, geese on the wing,
Soaring larks singing, whilst daffodils bloom.
Blossom on trees, petals falling like snow.
Lambs' tails of hazel pulsate in the breeze,
'Midst shady glades primrose and violets show.
Carpets of bluebells sway 'neath the trees,
Deep in the hedgerows where young lives abound,
Fox cubs from dark earths frolic in the sun,
Web spinning spiders, insects flit around,
Great tan-brown hares stand boxing as in fun,
March winds gusting, soft warm April rains,
Delights of spring down Yorkshire's country lanes.

E M Fearnley

NIGHT IN A NORTHERN TOWN

Putting on her neon makeup,
but dressed in dowdy, tattered garb,
she waits for the night's first customers,
cruising the lonely streets
looking for excitement,
or simply entertainment.
While passing through
they thought they'd stop and view her
or even partake of her pleasures,
while she, at her brightest hour,
rules uncrowned queen of the northern night,
an ageing temptress,
earning what she can.

Tracy Atkinson

HOME (LAISTERDYKE)

Crumbling mill yards, skips toppled, bales strewn.
Cracked stone flags worn smooth with time.
Weed infested walls, fertilised with soot.
Redundant mill chimneys from grey landscapes climb.

Naked railway lines haunted by laughter and bubbling expectation
long gone, demolished with the friendly local station.
Giant gas cylinders hover nearby.
Their ghostly outlines changeable as the sky.

Litter, grit, dog shit.
Patches of green invaded by gypsies
amongst old stone cottages, dilapidated flats with pebble dash
                                                            crumbling,
windows boarded, stairways cracked.

Rusty monuments to greed and waste reach for the sky.
Locals stagger from pubs nearby.
With unseeing eyes, voices distorted
they blunder through plastic cones, 'The pavement's contorted.'

Kids scatter from stinking phone boxes
leaving wires ripped out.
Then charge through shattered bus shelters,
diamonds crunching underfoot.

Stunted trees bedecked with rasping plastic
vibrate as traffic roars past,
spewing poison fumes, drawing you in like elastic,
a blight to our ears and chest.

This squalor is my birthright, my life, me.
And I stay though free to roam.
Like the weeds I've put down roots.
Laisterdyke is my home.

Jean Dunbar

THE VALESMAN

Alone on the farm the grandfather was
always aworry the weather brought rain.
Inspecting fields met with disheartening loss,
in *finished* corners or long stretches lain.
Once these were known and told, he seemed resigned.
Back to the fire, he bowstrung his braces,
and stared out the two-ways glaze, that combined
framed fields' hoar-frosted tan with a face's
rinse of shine. Winter white hair grew hay-tussled
like a boy's. To shy but playful chuckle,
he had ground his own crop of offspring's ears,
and stubble-burned grandchildren's lobes, with mauling
fists. On sheep, thru' the dip, they faster sheared
than woollen hand-me-downs come off folks' backs.
Done threshing, granary-stepped he, hauling,
on his back, endless over-heavy sacks.

Richard Lung

THE EX-PAT

I was born on right side of hills
Or wrong side if you're from over here
I'd rather have red rose than white rose
But I moved for a sort of career.

Give me a hot pot instead of a pudding
No I won't eat cheese with my cake
It's Manchester not Leeds that's United
But it's in the land of the Tyke that I wake.

So if that's my lot then I'll take it
It's beginning to quite grow on me
For the land to the East of the Pennines
Is England's second county.

Mick Freeman

UNTITLED

Old Charlie shuffles down the street,
A tired old body on tired old feet,
His past is etched upon his face
Memories are there which he can't erase,
People who knew him in his prime
Knew when and where to draw the line
You would never know to see him now
He had the strength to pull a plough
It's all gone now, he's worn and beat
But a harder man you will never meet
So you that are young,
Standing tall and erect,
Show this lonely old man
A lot of respect.

K Hudson

RIBBLEHEAD VIADUCT

You were not always there; you had your birth
Within a scaffold's intricate cocoon,
From which you broke to span the peaty earth
Of Ribblehead with your sublime pontoon;
Today, your limbs are cracked and crazed with age
That faults your lofty-arching fenestration,
Shotblasted by the icy pelting rage
Of a hundred Pennine winters' penetration;
Your traffic dwindles and your cargoes leave,
Accountants toll your deathknell; so - goodbye?
Can past endeavour's sweat win no reprieve
Lest you, once born for profit, now must die
    Of loss - or linger, crumbling monument
      To mark the way we once called permanent?

Philip Dacre

OUR YORKSHIRE HERITAGE

Yorkshire, England's largest county
Proudly gives us of its bounty -
County of great variation,
Some man-made, some God's creation.
Northwards, moors with purple heather
Compensate for winter's weather,
Southwards travelling o'er the wolds
Fields of grain in many gold's,
In between the dales lie snugly,
All is beauty, nothing ugly.
Further south and t'wards the west
Industrial towns give of their best
And coal and wool, to name but two,
Created wealth for quite a few,
But hardship and long hours for others
Until they organised as Brothers.
Yorkshire's sired some famous men,
Experts in sport or with the pen,
Engineers and sailors too,
In every field their *grit* wins through.
From the Romans, Norman's, Danes
We've acquired some funny names,
But still retained our own identity,
Dialects and characters in plenty
And then, the brightest star of all,
Nearly surrounded by its wall,
Our lovely ancient city - York,
Best enjoyed by those who walk
Around its narrow twisting streets,
And our Minster others beats,
If you are Yorkshire born and bred,
Although on foreign soil you tread,
You'll always hanker after *home*
Explore a bit then no more roam,
If you were raised on Yorkshire pud,
Then Yorkshire heritage is good.
Phoebe Roberts

SOUTH YORKSHIRE

South Yorkshire
is a county
that is well
worth knowing.
Its features
are a bounty
that merit
a showing.
South Yorkshire
can proffer
a star
studded city
when we say
we've lots to offer.
We are not
a Walter Mitty
our arena
brings singers
of world
wide fame
our pool
brings swimmers
for an
Olympic game.
Soon there'll be
a Supertram
to help us defeat
a traffic jam.
We have had
our ups and downs
with some major
trade slumps
but, like
other big towns
we are not
down in the dumps.
Winifred Heeley

SHEFFIELD - NOW AND THEN

Sheffield! - indeed the very name
Conjures up a city full of ills -
A dirty picture in a golden frame
Bordered by the Derbyshire Peak hills.

And to anyone who visits now
This picture never could have been so true,
Outsiders surely must be wondering how
The locals ever manage to get through.

At present deep holes decimate our roads,
Pedestrians and drivers all detour
And cranes and lorries now discharge their loads
Of pipes, to carry water, gas and power.

For very soon we'll have the Supertram
And roads and pipes must first all be prepared,
So while, just now it's one big traffic jam,
One day it will be worth these troubles shared.

We Sheffielders are proud of our great city
With long traditions of the world's best steel
Of knives and forks both functional and pretty
And Yorkshire folk with courage strong and real.

Our heritage is flat capped men in mills
Sweating as white hot steel pours to the ground
And buffer girls laughing away their ills
Though dust, disease and dirt were all around.

We rose up from the ashes of the blitz,
We showed our strength and we remained unbowed
And we rebuilt our city bit by bit
A city of whose children could be proud.

No more a dirty picture as before
Clean air replaced the murky factory smoke -
Something good that came out of the war
And *mucky* Sheffield just became a joke.

So, though we have a grumble and a moan,
We Sheffielders have lots of sports and fun,
We're proud this city is where we call home -
We'll just be glad when all this roadwork's done.

Doreen Wright

YORK

Three thousand years of vibrant life,
Has changed this low lying place,
Into a city alive with history,
Which has shaped the destiny
Of the world.

From here Constantine was proclaimed,
Who changed Europe to Christian belief,
And forged the basis of
World civilisation,
Today.

Here warlike Vikings lived and
Acquired a taste for home,
While through the middle ages
A mighty church rose whose
Awesome majesty rules supreme.

Here kings were bought and sold,
Senseless civil wars fought,
Merchants waxed fat,
The poor forgotten and
Men loved and died.

Today a tourist's dream,
Where people from all the world,
Can wonder at a past.
Which gives continuity and life,
To the future generations.

John Rayne-Davis

YORKSHIRE X 4

North, South, East or West,
which part of Yorkshire do you like best?
wide opened spaces of moorland ahead,
or
the sea of the North, all wild and angry -
where seagulls cry soundly
and cliffs crumble badly
or
you may like the centres all shiny
and new,
full of big shops and fun things to do.
The history may grab you in York Minster Abbey,
where deacons and arch deacons of
past years lay sleeping.
The Romans built walls around this
great, big city.
The ghosts of the past cry
'Oh! What a pity.'
But fear not come and see -
'cause Yorkshire is here for
you and for me.

Angela Feather

THE LAST SHIFT

Every morning when I awake
I put on my shirt and tie,
Every morning it's just the same
And I simply don't know why.

For as I arrive all tidy and neat
I wish it was different today
For I don't go to work all happy
Just sad, for now I know how long I'll stay.

So as I go through the old battered yard,
And past the old tumbling sign
I think of when the cogs did turn
And production was on the line.

But I'll remember well in years to come
When I used to enjoy these times
But Friday's arrived and the cogs have stopped
At the last of Yorkshire's mines.

Monique C Richardson

SCARBOROUGH

The sea wind blew heavy upon our beautiful Yorkshire coast,
The seagulls hovered sideways forced by the fisherman's ghost,
Like a sickening disease it created corrosion,
It devastated Holbeck like a silent explosion.

But the view of the harbour makes it possible to forget
For only good things are remembered from this water inlet,
Our castle stands proud, a great relic from the past,
Like our fishing tradition it will always last.

They say fishermen are created long before they are born,
Beyond their mortal years they leave widows to mourn,
Yet, the sea can be cruel and the hours linger on,
But it doesn't deter them from singing the seafarers song.

Ignominious battalions of lover roam our golden sands,
Cherished memories nil forgotten, as they read their wedding bands,
'Twas then I realised, I'd compared my wife to the sea,
Mysteriously quixotic, yet ever faithful to me.

Born unknown into the ancestral fisherman's web,
Until judgement day when existence proceeds the ebb,
My wife bore our children, a son and two daughters,
Once gone my spirit shall guide them through destiny's
                                    troubled waters.

Robert Messruther

THE VALLEY

The vale lies deep in Pennine Hills
Neath steeps protecting woollen mills
And viewed from t' tops upon the Moss
Trapped waters gleam in hollowed heights.
The gentle Holme descending there
Runs by old cottages to where,
The little town of *Summer Wine*
Sits astride her stony banks.
Familiar now to many folk
Are local scenes through which I walk
And I oft linger for a while
Near Nora's cot beside the rill.

I sip my coffee thinking now
Of olden times, so quiet, and how
As youngsters we would oft complain
'There's nowt to do in Holmfirth town,'
We thought that Huddersfield was *great*
Compared to life round Hollowgate.
Now strangers think it wonderful,
Their cameras click the whole day long.
And somehow this small Pennine town,
Which as a child could make me frown,
Is very precious to me now,
It seems so *Yorkshire* - and it's home!

Bess Beecroft

JACKDAWS ROUND ST LEONARD'S SPIRE

Round St Leonard's spire they fly,
jackdaws in the evening sky,
dipping, wheeling, rising high,
look with beady, glancing eye.
Jack, Jack, Jack, their calling cry.

Upthrust air in gusty flow
toss the jackdaws from below,
black stretched wings they plane, stoop low
astride the wild wind fast and slow.
Jack, Jack, Jack, call as they go.

Joyously they never tire,
jackdaws have but one desire,
lark and play, fly higher, higher
lit by setting sun's red fire
Jack, Jack, Jack, round St Leonard's spire.

Round and round St Leonard's spire
Jack, Jack, Jack, the sun's on fire!

Mary Newton

YORKSHIRE

Sitting on rocks high above the dales
How lucky I am to have this panamoric sight.
There is no better than God's groups of trees,
Or meandering streams bubbling below the height
Of steep fall hills dotted with sheep and barns.

The drystone walls complete the Yorkshire picture
Of country life and calmness, as of yore . .
And people living in a friendly vein -
What could one ask of civilisation more
Than happiness, fulfilment, and well-being?

These people have not turned to graft and business.
They are the farmers the very salt of the earth.
Their lives are full of work and hearty living
Keeping the people healthy and strong, from birth . . .
Until we die from stressful fight for life.

Joy Duggleby

MALHAM

He chose a ledge of lichen freckled rock to set his tripod up,
and through a complex, scientific machine, surveyed the scene.
Webs of white limestone
linking field with fell,
green Anglian terraces in serried rows, the brook tumbling below.

Hostile, bedraggled rams tore at coarse stubble bordering the rock,
with twitching hoof alert for lamb or ewe daring to venture near.
Birds wheeled in fright,
a hawk's shrill scream cleaved
the space, between this alien presence and the sheer cliff face.

Malham is one of time's great monuments - here nature alone
                                                                                 decides
where thorn, or birch, or oak should root in boulder clay, or where
the caverns be formed,
streams rise and flow.

The cove, unchallenged in a thousand years must stay,
let no man interfere.

M Platts

THE RIDINGS

It's not so very long ago, tha knaws,
White'all got a bee in its 'ead;
East Rahdin should break off from Yorrksher.
'O'er our dead bodies!' they said.
'O'd 'ard,' said the folk o' East Rahdin
'Tha mu'nt muck abaht wi' what's rheet
An' 'Umbersahde ain't *'ere* abidin'
It suits more for yon sugar beet!'
So now T'Local Gov'mnt Commission
Has adjusted its thinking cap
And made *West Rahdin'* shaped like a banana
And 'arrogate's all in a flap!

Ursula M Badger

SCARBOROUGH CASTLE

Above a gull be-spattered cliff you stand
Battered and bruised.
As if the fierce, grey waters
Churning at your feet
Had grasped with icy fingers
To fashion and refashion what other hands had once begun.
No swarthy Romans tread your halls today,
Nor sentries search with eagle eye
For bright-sailed dragon ships
To cleave the wind-whipped waters of the bay.
Haunted by wraiths of men long gone
Yet ever proud and beautiful
You still remain
An ancient guardian of our Yorkshire land.

Jess Chambers

IMAGES IN STONE

Stone is the essence of our town
Once, black as soot, the mills
And banks and chapels seemed
As everlasting as the hills
Which ringed the town.

Now mills are mostly raised,
Banks, glass and granite slabs,
Chapels adapted for commercial use.

What stone remains, washed pale as bone
Reveals carved fantasies for long unseen
Of shuttles, spindles, spiders,
Teasels, maddes, cottonplants, rams' heads,
forgotten bearded worthies and the Queen.

Barbara France

FROM A YORKSHIRE TYKE

I was born and bred in Yorkshire
It's divided into three,
There's North, South and West Ridings
No finer place to be.

The city of York with its Minster
There, stood on hallowed ground
Circled by its Roman wall
No better, could be found.

Its rivers, its dales, a pleasure to see
The cafés, boathouses, where you can have tea,
The Aire and the Calder, the Ouse and the Nidd
No money can buy, so don't even bid.
You can go the world over
By air, land or sea,
But here home in Yorkshire
You're longing to be.

As time passes by
And God looks for me,
Well, down here in Yorkshire
that's where I will be.

Samuel Fullwood

SPRING SONG

All night the angry wind has raged
But now our quiet woods are still.
On sodden earth the fallen leaves have caged
All signs of life, but soon tight buds will spill
Their tender green, and shake soft catkins in a pollen cloud
Pale sun will light the shadowy trees.
We need no more dark winter's clammy shroud
Fresh scents and sounds move softly on the breeze
Joyfully we know our northern spring is here.

Mary Found

HAPPY IN HEBDEN

The trailing clouds, the purple heather.
The open moors, the Pennine weather.
So happy in Hebden. No worries.

The boulder cloughs, the clapper bridges.
The waterfalls to singing rivers.
So happy in Hebden. No worries.

The packhorse tracks, the weavers trails.
The chimney stacks, in wooded vales.
So happy in Hebden. No worries.

The hilltop farms, the skylarks singing.
The rocky craggs, the hawk is hanging.
So happy in Hebden. No worries.

The beautiful earth and the beautiful skies
Hebden bridge is a natural high.

The old canal, the painted barges.
The horse-drawn boats, the floating arches
So happy in Hebden. No worries.

The cobbled streets, the sandstone paving
The Walkley Cloggs, the brass bands playing
So happy in Hebden. No worries.

The drystone walls, up and down houses.
The old mill shops, the corduroy trousers
So happy in Hebden. No worries.

The local folk, the new off-comedons.
The ageing hippies, the tourist humdrum.
So happy in Hebden. No worries.

The beautiful earth and the beautiful skies
Hebden bridge is a natural high.

Bryan Green

NORTH YORKSHIRE MORNING

Earth smell, green scent, wet leaf, misty morn.
Still lake, with bird calls, dragonfly with silvered wing.
Bullrush and lilypad, skylarks that rise and sing.

Cornfield and hedgerow, poppy flower like drop of blood.
Oak tree and willow, pheasant at the edge of wood.

Wooden bridge with hollow ring, furrowed path and weedy dyke.
Languid cows with glassy gaze, distant hills in purple haze.

D Hair

HEBDEN BRIDGE

When I was a child, I loved this town,
Hebden Bridge was home to me.
Going away was pleasant enough
But Hebden was where I longed to be.

I loved the shops, where, over the years,
My mum and dad had become well-known.
It was nice to go in and be hailed as a friend,
For Hebden Bridge was always home.

I went off to London and left it behind,
My town and my people remained.
But the longing for home never went from my mind,
For Hebden, my Hebden, was home.

Everything's changed now: more tourists, more folk,
More traffic, more bustle, more noise.
I'm older myself, and resistant to change,
But I'm back in my Hebden, my home.

Fay Fielding

THE MINER

In the bowels of the earth,
Toils a man for all his worth.
The richness of the *black diamond* field,
Gives little to him of its yield.
His masters down the ages have wrought
Havoc! With his life, his very thought,
He sweats, he toils with all his might,
Muscles glistening in the dim light.
His lungs are full of dust and grime,
The body scarred with the task and time.
He dices with death, but shows no fear,
A soldier in that vast inter.
In the darkness of the pits,
With little oxygen he sits.
The eerie groans of pressure on steel,
Just imagine, how he must feel?
He meditates, takes nourishment,
Is this work or punishment?
His soul is deeply wounded too,
Yet a man amongst men, a true blue.
The anguish of his-next-of-kin,
Will he come home, less a limb?
When the stint is finally done,
He arrives at the top, looks up at the sun,
Takes in the air, with a deep sigh of relief,
Thanks God! For his mates, his rest, and belief.

Charles Roshy

SEE

See all the beauty around you
And lock it within your heart
And whene'er a dark cloud pass o'er you
Remember that place in your heart.

Margaret Northern

A COUNTRY LANE IN AUTUMN

Pale sunshine filters
through the early mists
silvering delicate threads
of spiders' webs
which curtain hedges
in the morning dew.
Gathering by afternoon
a golden strength
it highlights the red-gold
glory of the trees
whose leaves in dying
give beauty a second birth
in vibrant tones of russet
yellow and bronze.
Poised like living creatures
they postpone their death
till whisked from branches
by a playful breeze.
Dizzy from dancing
they settle, layer on layer
a carpet of crackling pleasure
for children's feet.

Margaret Gott

NATURE'S TRAIL

The blistering sun beats down on me
As I yield to nature's dream
Ambling along her wilderness trail
Her presents, I redeem

The rustic glow of swaying ferns
Rustling in the breeze
Slender grasses piercing the air
Clasping the shade from the trees

Electric pylons span the sky
Stemming its tidal flow
Spanning the withering, bare limbed oak
The tiny, cowering plants below

Stubby, shortened hedgerows
Engulfing the freshly ploughed fields
The gasping jogger treading concrete earth
As to temptation, he yields

Quietly I walk this lonely path
Recapturing blissfulness
Then slowly returning to my suspect world
Filled with less happiness.

Pam Reynolds

HUDDERSFIELD MY TOWN

West Yorkshire is the place to be
For lots of people including me
Home is where the heart is
That's West Yorkshire for me.

Our shopping centre is quite good
With lots of variety of goods
An indoor and open market place
For bargain hunters it's just great.

Lots of cafes to have a meal
A sports centre of activity
Amusement centre and bingo hall
A cinema if you care to call.
Friendly people, helpful too
Got a sense of humour too
Who could ask for more
Than being Yorkshire born?

Lily Mansfield

DREAMING

Even though we're far apart
I've still got you in my heart.
All the memories that we shared
Even though you never cared.
Time's supposed to heal the pain
When all it does is make me cry again.
When I think of that very day
When I was sleeping, dreaming away.
I don't know why or when, I fell asleep
But when I woke, you were at my feet.
We walked alone hand in hand
Our bare feet touching the cool, damp sand.

Shadows cast across the sea,
All I could see were you and me.
Here I was in holiday bliss
I'll always remember our very first kiss.
In the darkness of the night
Under the pale moonlight.
I wouldn't give up without a fight
But the sea got my mind
The answer I could not find.

Emma Ward (14)

A TREASURED LIFE

Speak of the shire of York
And it brings to mind
That place you dread to leave
And the place you always want to return

Speak of the shire of York
See the moors tumbling into the coast
And the coast tumble into the sea
Reaching far out to eternity

Speak of the shire of York
Wrapped up in so much history
And the greatness
Of the past, present and future

Speak of the shire of York
Of the people who live and breathe Yorkshire
In rural or industrial scene
No better to be found

Speak of the shire of York
Look no further for that heaven on earth
You entered, you enjoyed and will finally leave
But oh! What a treasured life
In the shire of York.

Hilary Wood

UNTITLED

Mexborough, a town in South Yorkshire,
where everyone worked at the mine.
For fifty-one years down at Manvers
dad worked, come rain, hail or shine.

In the 50s when neighbours were friends too,
no-one feared to go out in the dark,
mother unconcerned about daughter,
who just shouted, 'I'm off to the park.'

The clippies who worked on the trackless,
after a hard day's graft.
If us youngsters had threatened to rob them,
they'd have kicked our backsides and then laughed!
Now, there's no congregation of youngsters
no pictures and no skating rink.
Just computers and video nasties,
where will it all end? Meks yer think!

D Beardsley

THE CHOCOLATE BAR

I sat there waiting for the bus,
the one I'd missed had made me cuss.
A well-dressed lady sat down by my side,
we said *hello* as we waited to ride.
All of a sudden, out of the blue,
came a loud yell from a woman she knew.
'Hi ya, are yer alreight flower?
I've come fo't bus thet gus on't our.
And as she spoke she just kept eating,
her chocolate bar as she made her greeting.
At her side her friend now stood,
and started to speak - as I thought she would.
I had a shock, I'd thought she was posh,
one of those ladies with plenty of dosh . . .
'Eh Elsie, if thy eights all that lot,
thal ev ne teeth, the'l all ev rot.'
The answer she got was just so funny,
it made my grey day, very sunny.
'Nay od on luvvy, dun't worry lass,
I just tek em art, and inta't glass!'

Marion Warke

FREE TODAY

September 19th was an eventful day
When Selby Bridge Toll was taken away
Selbians thought this day would never be
Or they would never live to see
After 100 years of Selby Bridge pay
Motorists could drive over it free today.

In the town it was an occasion
Flags were hung on the bridge for decoration
Lord Mayor and councillors were there
Crowds of people who wanted to share
The ceremony of the last toll
So the traffic could freely roll.

Now we are waiting for a bypass
Then we hope that heavy traffic at last
Will be diverted from the centre of town
No more traffic jams to cause any harm
More trade and work for everyone
Then Selby town will be well run.

Hilda Mary Regan

A SONG

I'll sing you a song about steel,
I'll sing you a song about coal.
I'll sing you a song about working folk
Who've never heard of dole.

I'll sing you a dirge for those bygone days,
I'll sing a lament for the past.
I'll sing you a song if you'll listen my dear
I'll sing it through it be my last.

The song that I sing it must be a sad song
For singing is all I can do.
There isn't a job for a working man
When he's over forty-two.

Yes, me and my mates from down at the works
Are redundant and thrown out to rot,
And where the factory used to stand
A shopping mall marks the spot.

So I'm here in the rain - a one-man band,
And I sing in a tone slightly flat.
As I watch the workers passing by
I say to myself, 'I could do that.'

Gi' us a job.

Lynda Billard

SHEFFIELD

What is it like I hear you ask?
Well to live in Sheffield is quite a task
The buses go everywhere but where they should
The cars drive on roads that go thud, thud, thud
Long live the Supertram, it's Sheffield's gem
Or so we've been told by invisible ad men

Now that I've got that moan off my chest
I'll get to the subject of Sheffield's best
Our theatres and galleries they rival the west
To each foreign traveller what to do is a test
The Lyceum, the Crucible, Don Valley too
A great wealth of history old and some new
Sheffield you cannot cling to your past
'Little mesters' redundant, steel's ground its last
Coal lies forsaken seams high as black towers
Remember and go on before the dream sours
Sheffield people are proud, stout Yorkshire folk
Their motto is simply, 'Why fix what ain't broke'?

Claire Robinson

BYGONE TRAINS

The slow train to Barnsley
Is ready to leave - would you believe?
Jerks grudgingly forward, convulses and heaves
Leaving Rotherham at quarter to ten
Late once again.
Black smoke and coal fumes and steam all combine
To ruin the washing on many a line
Many a line, many a line,
Stopping at Rowmarsh at Swinton and Wath
Changing at Cudworth and cursing in wrath.
Carrying miners and farmers and husband and spouse
This was the slow train to Barnsley Court House.

Siren!
Trans Pennine electric in dark blue and gold, dashing and bold
Train of the future once we were told,
Blue sparks sizzle the overhead wire, overhead wire,
Gone is the fire, gone is the smoke,
No need to stoke,
Silently gliding through Guide Bridge and Dinting
Cutting, butting, jutting, sprinting,
Over the heather, over the moor,
Woodheads hooded tunnelled floor,
Woodheads hooded tunnelled floor,
Woodheads hooded tunnelled floor,
Dashing though Mill Town and Lakeland and river
Gone!
Gone in an instant and now gone forever.

Roy Blackman

THE YORKSHIRE THAT I LOVE

The rare, pretty wild flowers,
The heather on the moors,
The old steam locomotives,
The sheep on the valley floors.
The sandy coastline beaches,
The wind whistling through my hair.
The Monolith at Rudston,
Cautious animals taking care.
The foxes and the badgers,
The forests and the woods,
The farmers working hard,
The weather and the floods.
The grey and ancient churches,
The rivers and the streams,
The fields and the commons,
The cheeses and the creams.

Thomas Wells (8)

LEISURE TREASURE

Some go to sunny Malta,
Some the Dodeconese,
To Cyprus, Crete, Minorca,
And islands such as these.
But of all these distant places
There are none that can compare
To Yorkshire's rural beauty.
And bracing, pure, fresh air.
Some think foreign is essential.
But have they yet explored
North Yorkshire's full potential?
Our Ridings' golden hoard?
Yorkshire has everything of the very best.
And Scarborough is the crowning jewel
In Yorkshire's bounteous treasure chest.

V Clarke-Irons

SCARBOROUGH

The gulls have wheeled round the cliffs, their aching crying

Witnessed the fall of faraway Rome,
And the Saxon Harold's dying.

Since the Romans built their signal station
Since Skarthi built his burg,
Since Britain became a nation,
Through World Wars, prosperity and unemployment,
Scarborough folk have endured,
Against the breeze that blows endlessly from the sea,
Mocking the garish halls dedicated to computer games,
While green still rings the town and climbs the hills,
Looking out to water where German guns once spat flames.

Over all this,
The gulls have screamed their aching cry,
Around the cliffs, around the people,
And the waves rolling in from the water desert of the sea.
While under the castle huddle the people of the Shires, we
Who endure the shock, the years, the wind, the surge
Of the water from which the trawlers still wrest the fish
Stubborn folk who maintain the flow of life, the urge,
To survive in the sea winds, the flood of time,

Huddled in squat terrace houses, and bare fishermen's bars,
These Yorkshire people endure
Under the gaze of the gulls and the light of the indifferent stars.

Jeremy Ward

FILEY BAY

Trippers visit for the day
To bask on sands at Filey Bay,
Walk the Ravine a verdant scene
Cool haven as a tranquil dream.

The Coble Landing to explore
The fishing boats they do adore,
Amusements and the shellfish stalls
While above the waves a seagull calls.

The finger point of Filey Brigg
Around it, the Yachting Club do jib,
At ebb of tide the rock pools fill
And all about, the air is still.

So if you delight in simple charms
Of beach, and hearing fishermen's yarns,
Hope you will come enjoy a stay
And sample life at Filey Bay.

Glenda Lawrence

HOME COUNTY

This Yorkshire of mine,
    a county so fine -
Is the place I love best,
    it's my memory chest.
From coast to inland,
    the scenery's grand -
With the moors and the dales,
    their beauty never fails.
There's industry too,
    famous buildings to view,
And famous people, now gone
    but their names linger on.
And though things may change
    in life's varied range -
It's still home to me -
    and where I like to be -
        Yorkshire.

Doreen Wilson

ODE TO A NORTHERN TOWN

Carnival blossom
The size of postage stamps
Tickertapes a kind of
Welcome, along the mizzled street.
Pink, and white, and orange moon confetti.

'Please, please, please,
Let me be anywhere, but here,'
They say, 'Anywhere but looking at
These dark houses and sad faces.
The chip shop papered street,
The peeling *Laura-loves-Daz* bus-shelter.'

'Let us be in sunnier sites,
Exotic climes, surrounding
Happier faces. India or Ceylon,
- Barbados would do.

Waves lapping at our feet, the
Feel of space, the movement
Of air around us.'
'We would come back, we would, we would,
We really, really would . . .'

Bloody liars.

Helen Burke

MEMORIES

We would play amongst the bracken,
        my brother, Chris, and I.
We rested on the heather
        and watched the sheep go by;
And when it came to lunchtime
        the tame ones gathered round.
They rummaged through our picnic,
        eating anything they found.
We would run down to the station
        at the same time every day
To watch the people come and go
        and wave them on their way.
They really were a splendid sight,
        those trains long out of date.
We had our favourite one of course,
        old 80118.
Then, if our day was not filled up
        and we had time to spare
We'd race up to the Village Stores
        and buy some chocolate there.
Here once again in Goathland
        the past comes back to me;
Those holidays of childhood
        when the sun shone endlessly.

Marion Elliott

BARNSLEY

Barnsley town is a Yorkshire place,
Strong on character, low on grace.

Its folks have known times good and hard,
Village greens and terrace backyard.

Prosperity, once through here passed,
What remains is shrinking fast.

Its people are to their lot resigned,
They still are warm and blunt and kind.

Forged by hardships through the years,
Bleak as winter their ideas.

Linen, glass and coal have been,
Little trace can now be seen.

Packhorse trails, canals and railways,
More like memories than highways.

Grand outdoor markets on most days,
Have been replaced by concrete bays.

Old, narrow, busy, crowded streets,
Once were filled with sensory treats.

Today those streets are paved with brick,
Shop fronts once homely now look slick.

Stalls of bargains, choice and plenty,
Replaced by dear, alike or empty.

Cinemas, parks and pubs often full,
The crowds they can no longer pull.

For now we're holding back a bit,
We all know our fire's still lit.

No need to show our hopes, our fears,
We've known each other many years.

As workers we will bear each chore,
Some day our sun will shine once more.

Patrick Sykes

OUR EARTH

Earth unfetter'd deep and dark, depths below
cruel, stark, unrelenting as the wave
you hold the secret of the brave,
of men who toil below your crust
who, buy your coal, who breathe your dust.
Bodies lithe, ears alert, *instinct* to those who
with you work. Many men have known you
years, grown familiar, lost their fears.
Yet even so has come the day, whey you have
claimed them as your prey. Your yoke is
not an easy one, the race with you is never
won, the grass so green that hides your lust
or rain that dampens your surface dust; or
snow that makest you so white, or dark that
puts you out of sight.
Do they know your mighty power, do they know your hungry hour?
Many lands have seen your jaws,
You who knows not any laws.

O earth so cruel. Yet so kind
for everything in you we find.

Cecil Wadsworth

A YORKSHIRE POEM

Yorkshire's the county,
The best in the land,
With moors, farms and castles,
And scenery so grand.

With small sleepy villages,
Hidden from view,
And quiet streams, and forests,
So old, yet so new.

With the Minster at York,
And the sea, not too far,
The history of Whitby,
And the Harrogate Spa.

The beautiful racecourses,
Scattered around us,
The food, and the beer,
Both filling and gorgeous.

The high rolling moors,
With the sheep, and the heather,
The hot sunny days,
In the beautiful weather,
The churches, museums,
And thick Roman walls,
The water cascading,
Down Aysgarth's old falls.

With racehorses working
In teams, on the Wolds,
With a backdrop of fields
Rolling endless in folds.

With stone walls, and rivers,
Fine fish in the lakes,
With boating, and swimming,
We have most things it takes
To have heaven on earth,
It's all here, you can see,
There's no place like Yorkshire,
At least, not for me.

Walter Smith

TIMES ON THE HAMBLETON HILLS 1940-1944

How is it when in silhouette against the sky,
I see the outline of a hill, but passing high,
That from my lips - from deep my heart - escapes a sigh
For times gone by?

How can it be that yet - to inner me
Leap scenes of springy turf, lake, blue moths, scree -
Winds, woods, wild flowers - the grey fox wilily
Still loping free?

Sandy sheeptracks vanish round a shoulder -
We scramble over fallen rock and boulder
To where, upon the cliff, the wind is colder
And mosses moulder.

So - though the times are gone when we adventured, wild and free
And though new times now leave their mark on old-time scenery,
Across the hills from our time flies a swift-winged bird to me -
Our memory.

Gwenda L Mather

HOUGHTON WOODS (EAST RIDING OF YORKSHIRE)

Slowly in the haze of heat
I climb the path to the woods.
Into the silvery sand my feet
Sink without sound.
And all around
Under a chequered coverlet
Of fields, the earth lies strangely quiet.

In the jewelled gloom of trees
I stand. Straight and palely green
Grow woodland plants. There's no breeze.
Each slender spire
Mute with desire,
Silently reaches for the sky.
And I found peace as I went by.

Jean Blackburn

YORKSHIRE

The Yorkshire Moors are world renowned.
In song we sing of *Ilkla Moor ba ta't*.
More famous still are Haworth Moors
where Catherine still seeks her Heathcliffe.

The Bronte name lives on forever.
Is it because of their literary genius
or, because of their short, tragic lives?
I believe it is because of the beautiful Yorkshire Moors.

They are in your heart.
They are in your soul.
A rich, rugged landscape of heathered moors
mingling with dykes of magnificent Yorkshire stone.

S C Riley

BYGONE BRADFORD

Tall, black chimneys line the sky
reminders of the times gone by
down cobbled streets to mills we went
little money to be spent.
Chimney sweeps all covered in soot
some folks thought they brought good luck
happy kids playing whip and top
ha'penny of sweets from corner shop
Friday night out comes tin baths
no hot water from the taps
buckets of water on to boil
on the fire a shovel of coil
kids scrubbed clean and sent to bed.
Mam gets busy baking bread
these days long gone such a pity
but it's still a grand place Bradford city.

B McGough

YORKSHIRE

Yorkshire is the place for me,
It boasts magnificent scenery,
Beautiful hills and waterfalls,
Winding rivers, old stone walls,
Rambling fells, heathered moors,
Valleys green craggy shores,
Historic towns and castles old,
Ruined abbeys and cities bold,
Haunting woods, unspoilt villages,
Waterways with famous bridges,
Dialect broad and cheery faces,
The friendliest people, the best of places.

Lynette Griffiths

UNTITLED

I love North Yorkshire, the land of my birth
With its broad acres and rich, fruitful earth
its moors and its valleys and dales so green
Where cattle and sheep so peaceful are seen.
There are many villages with old cottages and church
Where craftsmen are living engaged in their work.
There are country shows and crowds congregate
To view all the produce the villagers make.
The ruined monasteries which King Henry destroyed
To fill all his coffers his foul deeds were deployed.
Some beautiful houses of historic fame
And descendants still living guarding their name.
The ancient buildings, the Minster and walls you can walk
To see all the sights in the city of York.
The people, the memories, the land and the sea
There's never a place like North Yorkshire for me.

Florence Watson

NORTH RIDING RESURRECTION

Gaunt ridge of sculpted snow-cave guards the ice-track
slow-laden branches sweep the forest floor
grey-leaden skies merge seas without horizon
bleak north winds howling scour the barren moor

In the tall wood the trees are arcing columns
in the torn hedge the wild-rose blood is sprayed
in the turned field the aching furrow deepens
in silver sleep the earth is racked and flayed

Clean bones of moorland curve the low-slung skyline
grey braids of stone walls bind the winding lane
filigree frost delights each burnished fern leaf
from crystal dreams the earth will turn again

In the slow thaw the trees are laced with diamonds
in the low sky the sun lies liquid gold
in the brown fold the emeralds spears are singing
in spring-lit-jewelled-laughter curls the world

Chrysalis leaves of beeches break and glisten
cream-foaming elder flower crowns the lane
meadow and hedgerow, bridlepath and woodland
with honeysuckle veils transfigure pain.

Daphne Parker

MOVE OVER, WORDSWORTH!

There are bombs in Northern Ireland; there's famine in the world,
And the economic situation's grey;
On the mat below the letterbox there lie the usual bills,
But - the daffodils are out along the Stray!

If I were realistic, I'm told, I'd feel depressed
And despair would be the order of the day;
But the sun is out this morning, and the air is clear and cold,
And the daffodils are out along the Stray!
So *you* moan about the Centre, *you* fret about the rates,
And the broken paving-stones along the way;
You'll forgive *me* if I turn my mind to more important things,
Like the daffodils that bloom along the Stray.

Yes, I know these daily worries are enduring facts of life,
The dragons we are called upon to slay;
But we fight with better courage when our spirits are sustained
By the daffodils that bloom along the Stray.
And when the strife is over, and we know as we are known,
And the trivial cares of living fall away,
Do you think that Gabriel's horn will furnish half so brave a sight
As that blaze of golden trumpets on the Stray?

Bill Stanton

OUR TOWN

Bingley awakened to the blackbirds call,
where stands Myrtle Park to greet one and all.
The River Aire was so clear and bright,
rippling and gurgling in dawn's early light.
Wandering and weaving its happy way,
to greet the dawning of a brand new day.

Trinity Church spire clasped the dawn to its breast,
while the sparrows busily built their spring nests.
Mouse Wood and Alter Rock looked proudly down,
on this Bingley of ours, our own little town.
Fine trees lined our Main Street, meticulous and neat,
their pink blossom falling to lie at our feet.

Shop upon shop stood bright and shinning and clean,
with wares sold by hand now forgotten, unseen.
Clanking trolleys meandered their way down the tracks,
from Crossflatts to Saltaire, then all the way back.
The boats on the river gave enormous pleasure,
memories to hold and forever treasure.

Myrtle Park gave lots of fun,
with many a happy hour spent in the sun.
Kids ran wild, sunburnt and content,
While of an evening we teenagers to the Prinny went.
The Myrtle and Hipperdrome held many delights,
pictures that thrilled you night after night.

Folk streamed to the mills, their service to give,
twisting and spinning in order to live.
The Parish church bells would ring out a gay song,
on those calm summer evenings now long one.
Once more into darkness, night would fall,
with the Blackhills Wood standing guard over all.

Sparkling stars shone on our Bingley fair,
while the half hidden moon cast its bright glare.
This was our Bingley, the Bingley we loved,
nestling in the valley, contented and snug.
Long gone now, forgotten, forsaken, betrayed,
with plans for a new Bingley already made.

Knighton Joyce

SPRING STORM

Gathering clouds, discordant air in motion
Purple, black-flashed yellow moors.
Furious pageant of the elemental ocean
Pounding, beating senses arid shores.
The blue-black blanket, rain-fringed heaven
Edged by the gold of the obscured sun
Whose fingers touch the shadowed clinging heather
Through the moving curtain where the fabric's worn.
Not far behind this dark, chaotic veil
The valley basks in warmth and light,
Spectator to the storm that rolling, sails
Across the day to make it night.
Watch the heathland rise and swell in time
To heartbeat and the heavenly drums
Lifted in light, depressed in violet dark-shine,
Billowing quilt, celestially spun.
Licked by tongues of searing bright-light,
Silver scars of molten drystone walls
Thread their way, like silent snails in moonlight;
Shimmering traces of angel scrawl
Marking outcrop, stream, copse and dwelling,
Flickering seams to hold the earth
Against the seasonal, life-triumphant swelling
Of Mother Nature, celebrating birth!

Bez Hinnighan

A BEAUTIFUL PLACE

North Yorkshire is a beautiful place
With all its moors and heather
The only thing that lets it down
Is, of course, the weather.

There's many cities and villages
And lots of open space
Which all combine together
To make a special place.

In spring the place comes alive
With lots of pretty flowers
And visitors from miles around
Come, sit and gaze for hours.

Me, I like North Yorkshire
With all its charm and grace
That's why I find North Yorkshire
Such a beautiful place.

Clare Barnett

TEMPLE NEWSAM - LEEDS

Its place assured in history, the Great House stands serene,
The mellow brick, its mullions stone, the noble text written clear.
Here was born Lord Darnley who married Scotland's Queen
Their son King James both thrones ruled; United Kingdom founding
                                                                                     here.

This house and thousand-acre park of gardens, lakes and lovely
                                                                                      woods
Oasis peaceful: always green and crown of Leeds, its priceless
                                                                                  treasure.
A beauty we may all enjoy, and rest from stress in pensive moods,
A feast for eyes of nature's colour, release our minds from city
                                                                                 pressure.

Vandals degrade its woods, rubbish dump and burn-out cars:
But patiently the guardians remove, renew, repair,
To keep for us this paradise, surviving all our wars -
Tending shrubs, replanting, they toil with Adam's loving care.

Among the bracken in the woods I met the other day
A prisoner escaped, and free from rules enforced by men.
She picked her way so daintily, a happy clucking way,
Calm, sedate, bubbling joy and charming me - a small Rhode Island
                                                          hen!

Audrey Organ

REQUIEM
Closure of a coal mine and coke ovens in South Yorkshire

I loved your power,
Flame leaping from the stack,
Thick smoke around a mightiness
To last forever.

And after all the rites,
I thought you would have risen,
A paragon again
A Phoenix from the ashes.

Even the cattle noticed
Everybody did, they missed the noise
And warmth and friendliness,
The stark reality.

And now this quiet pride
Still-life against the sky,
There is no heartbeat any more,
People are in a row

And everything is neat and tidy.

Mary Wood

BEMPTON

Sheer white cliffs, that rise up from the sea
with sea birds nesting merrily.
The cliffs of Bempton are a marvellous sight
that fill the senses with delight.
The strength and grandeur of the scene below
with the churning sea washing to and fro.
I could feel the power, with emotions mixed
as I stood there on the cliffs - transfixed.
How insignificant we mortals are
when nature shows us from afar
her strength - as with an iron fist.
We are just powerless to resist
But the gentle side of nature's scene
were the seagulls gliding, so serene
Gracefully hovering oh, so high
performing a ballet in the sky.
the breeze that blew in from the sea
danced about, so happily.
Blowing the cobwebs all away
what a lovely exhilarating day.
I must return to feel once more
the happiness I felt, on that lovely shore.

Marjorie Corrie

YORK MINSTER

I sing a hymn
To substance
I sing a hymn
To the glory of God's accidents
I sing a hymn
To structure
I sing a hymn
To the three dimensions of material existence . . .

. . . But, in silence, I rise
To touch a fourth
And, in silence, I aspire
To the very point
Of human desire.

No-one may fulfil it,
But look - for a moment I still it.

Sean de Podesta

FISH

      That great, big, most gorgeously,
colourful fish never seems to even swim
close to me though I'm holding out
my fishing rod as far as it will go,
I'm almost falling over with the frustration and the woe.
      Then I look down at my feet,
knee-deep in water and I see all these
little fish through the salty waves,
and if I look closely I can pick out all
the different colours that shimmer and
gleam in the rippling waters pave.
      I toss aside my fishing rod and
though the water is cold I dive in head first,
to join the big school of little fish and
my tainted bubble is burst.
      I can see them all looking and
talking to me with bubbles of love I've never known,
I turn around and I realise the big fish is most alone.
      Then as I look back I see the small fish
have gone on ahead without me,
but I'll just swim swiftly on though
the water is cold and icy.
      For I yearn to believe in the life I have chosen,
because love's ongoing virtue echoes.

Delia Rutlidge

CURSED INTO BASTARDY

The headlines scream
The Ridings are back.
We all rejoice with glee.

The Ridings, North, East and West,
A thousand years of history.
The North Riding's pride
Dramatic moors and landed gentry.
Whilst in the East Riding
The Wolds roll to the sea.
The West Riding spawned mills,
Mines plus the iron and steel industry.
All three encircling York,
Our heart, the ecclesiastical see.
White Rose forever.
The greatest county.

But, where are we?
South Yorkshire.
At the stroke of a bureaucrat's pen
Cursed into bastardy.

Iris E Limb

OUR ENVIRONMENT

We live among the textiles
As well as engineering
In densely built-up areas
Not far from any clearing.

We have not far to go
To reach Yorkshire's beauty spots
Bolton Abbey, Barden Towers
Oh I could mention lots.

The rivers and streams pass you by
The air is fresh and clean
I doubt that in this world
You'd find a more environmental scene.

We haven't far to travel
To reach these breath taking views
As we who live in the West Riding
Regard this as history not news.

When God made our pleasant Riding
He did it to the letter
No matter where on earth you go
You could not find any better.

A G Ede

THE CITY OF LEEDS

The Town Hall at the centre of the city
The Civic Hall and the University
Post Office buildings and the Queen's Hotel
The Black Prince stands in the square as well.
Corn Exchange, Victoria Quarter
Granary Wharf right next to the water.
Woodhouse Lane and the BBC
Kirkstall Road and Yorkshire TV
Temple Newsam, Lotherton Hall
Roundhay Park we have them all.
City Varieties, The Playhouse, The Grand
No finer theatres in the land
Shall I go on? I've sown all the seeds
Surely you've guessed?
My home town is Leeds.

M Mason

UNTITLED

Yorkshire is a legend passed by word of mouth
To youngsters down the ages by the generation past.
They learnt about the customs and the toil of honest men,
About the pits, the mills, the fishermen, the farmers and, not last,
The families in houses, so very old and small
No sanitation, gardens, little food, where all was shared,
Where clothes were passed from child to child with some no shoes
                                                                                                at all.
Sickness was a nightmare, the remedies home-grown
No work - no pay, so none were ill until they almost died
But people worked at what they could and children laboured too
At any job which could be done 'twixt dawn and eventide.
So Yorkshire prospered through the years the people made it so.
A wealthy county built on wool, and coal, and faultless steel
Where strangers, come for moors and crags,
Grand beauty of the dales, are made to feel
That Yorkshire folk, the Yorkshire ways
Make Yorkshire great today.

M Staddon

A TASTE OF YORKSHIRE

Eh, lass, remember the days
when we were young,
and full of *put on* coquettish ways?

Remember the dances at the Palais Ballroom,
and how we were never short of a dance wi' the lads,
till we each took one as a groom?

Eeh, lass, did our lives change,
more so, when the bairns came along,
and we felt tied to the kitchen range?

And, oh, how soon our families grew and moved away,
how life's been full of changes,
and now lass, here we are, old and grey!

But you know, some things are still a fixture,
look into this bag and take your pick,
a fruit gum or a Yorkshire mixture?

Julia A Smith

BYGONE - BY'ECK

Steel giants once help up the clouds,
And lowered to hell my brave friends in cages,
Noise and danger met by valour unbowed,
Hard labour exchanged for their wages.

But those days and t'pits are gone, my son,
Their deaths marked by graves of levelled land,
Mourned by queues of men with no work to do,
Whose time rests so heavy on their hands.

Now they build huge shopping malls to reuse derelict land,
And Sheffield held the Student Games and will soon have a
                                                    Supertram,
But all of this newfangled glitz shows they'll never understand,
That this regeneration is just an economic sham.

Such innovations create few jobs and everybody knows,
That none of them can compensate for the industry of old,
Which now lives only in faded black and white photos,
And in my lifetime's memories which to you I've told.

Andrew J Massey

ME 'N' YORKSHIRE

Ah'll raise a glass t' Yorkshire
T' hills n't' dales n't' land
Ah'm thankful to old Yorkshire
It's made mi wot ah am
Ah'm proud to be a Yorkshire lass
Mi' family kith 'n' kin
All have Yorkshire blood inside
Now't purer will you find within
Sunday's always t' biggest treat
We sit rahnd fire 'n' toast us feet
We'll have roast beef 'n' Yorkshire puds
Cabbage, carrots 'n' loads a spuds
N' if, but ah doubt, should ah ivver wander
It wu'nt be long afore ah'm back dahn yonder
'Cos it wa Yorkshire made mi' strong
N' Yorkshire's mi' home, it's where ah belong
N' ah wu'nt ivver go away
Not nagh, not ivver, na mi' dyin' day.

Maureen Smith

BLACK HILL

The dip-slope has risen patiently,
mile after mile, up from the Humber and past High Flatts,
where once the energies of wind constantly
turned the autumn corn for winter's baps.

After a staggering slump into the last valley
it discovers water again, the trout rippled Holme.
Then with a huge heave, a final rally,
the slope rears up the Moss covered in cottongrass foam.

Heathered summit of the western thirding,
roof or our world, the only things above
are skylarks ascending and a towering
range of blueblack cumulus, buttressing
snow slopes of pale salmon blush.

Rippled spine of all England, from Peak
to Cumbria, tough as the sheep on its quilted hills.
Black plateau horizon under vermilion streaks,
shielding its people in their factory and mill.

Christine Ross

SILENCE OF THE TRAMS

Night-time in Hillsbro', the mist and gloom,
A feeling descends of dread and doom.
All around are huge, shadowy shapes,
Their necks are long and mouths agape.
What are these monsters of the night?
Are they vicious, do they bite?
The lights are out, it's so dark,
It seems just like Jurassic Park.
Are they dinosaurs I can see,
Leering in the dark at me?
Behind wire cages appear large holes,
As if dug out by some giant moles.
Mounds of earth reach to the sky,
Like weird volcanoes up on high.
There's disarray, North, East and West,
Is it some sort of endurance test?
Spielberg could make a film to show
The upheaval and the tales of woe.
How Sheffield beat the traffic jams,
And called it, 'The Silence of the Trams.'

Anne Sharman

BRIDLINGTON

Flat marshland
    taken over
High-rise flats home
    to sand weary kids.
Rock-pooled green crabs
    collected in wet sand
While tide was out.
Harboured boats groan
    paint starved
Another year; silver, wriggling fish
Stare blankly -
Oblivious to seaside appetites,
Yellow dash on sudden grey
'Copter and lifeboat avert distress.
Strength, skill, teamwork,
Yorkshire's heritage.

Irene Patricia Kelly

YORKSHIRE YEARNING

What can one say about Yorkshire moors,
this wasteland clad in purple heather,
where grasses stoop to howling tempests
and bursting becks half-hidden murmur?

It is a shire for hardened people
where humour lies in walls and valleys,
where hawthorn trees with seasons toughen
and birds with snow in winter battle.

And when the skies at last will mellow
to let the stars in blue-grey wander,
the hills can shape with mystic splendour,
despite the cold, the gloom, the silence . . .

Many will say the farms are dreary;
some will scoff at the still sheep leering;
but once this awesome air has stirred you,
the soul will always yearn for Yorkshire.

P J Krumins

LINES ABOUT A LINE

A grand, old Yorkshire character was my father's Uncle Jowt,
And the humorous things he said and did, my father told me about.
He had a longer, *posher* name, of that I have no doubt,
But to all who knew and loved him, he was simply known as *Jowt*.

There used to be a railway line from Holmfirth down to town,
Where the well-beloved *Holmfirth Express* puffed daily up and down.
In a 3rd-Class carriage, horsehair seats prickled above our socks,
But the platform's slot machine, for tuppence, issued a bar of chocs.

In the green fields by the railway line Jowt thought it made good
                                                              sense
To build a little poultry hut surrounded by a fence.
So he built his hut, put up the fence and the very self-same day
He bought a dozen White Leghorns, all guaranteed to lay.

His well-fed hens were laying well, but I'm very sad to say
The silly creatures had no sense and onto the line would stray.
The first of those poor, luckless hens to meet a tragic fate
Was cooked with sage and onion, ending on Jowt's dinner plate.

But after more fatalities, Jowt went down to the station
And to the stationmaster he explained the situation.
Said he, 'I can't go on like this, it's keeping me quite poor.'
So he got for the hens a timetable and stuck it on the henhouse
                                                              door.

Mildred Holmes

NORTH YORKSHIRE

Stone-built cottages in the dales,
ruined abbeys and folk tales,
miles and miles of drystone walls,
splashing torrents of waterfalls.
The river running swiftly by
heather moors stretching to the sky.
Sheep and lambs in pastures graze
contentedly on warm, spring days.
Cricketers play on the village green
a happy sunlit peaceful scene.
resorts that are bright and full of fun
deckchairs on beaches in the sun,
the cry of gulls, the crash of waves
splashing into the smuggler's caves.
Towering cliffs that dip down to the sea
this is what North Yorkshire means to me.

Ruth Margaret Rhodes

THE MILL

Wheels of time turn
leaving hidden by swollen rivers
reminders of industrial decay

Tall sandstone chimneys
stand reaching and proud
yet still

Once enemy to the bleak Pennine landscape
now cradled like a child within the undergrowth
of sleepy hills

For the Mill
life has gone

For the workers and their children
their echoes still remain
clad to the shapes of stone like moss.

Ron Lister

ANDY CAPP PUB PATTER

There's just one boss in wor hoose
Nee marra what folk think,
It's aalwis me thit caals the tune
Let's hev anouther drink.
Suppose aa dee can yem rollin drunk
She'll not hev nowt te say,
Aa think it's yor torn te get thim in
Afore we're on wor way.

Divvent taak te me aboot wimmins lib
Aa've hord it aal afore,
She wouldn't dor come that wi me
Or she'd be oot the door.
Gudneet lads see ye later
Ye cin bank on me.
Will ye open the door flower?
Aa've forgot me key.

Aa've browt ye a bottle of lager love,
Aa forgot te make yor home brew.
Aa've just been tellin the lads it the pub
Aa'll aa wud dee for ye,
Aa divvent knaa hoo ye put up wi me
Remembrin yor lager but forgetting me key.

Dorrie McMenemy

WHAT YORKSHIRE MEANS TO ME

I was born and bred in Bradford,
'Mid its dark, satanic mills,
But always at the weekend I'd wander in the Dales.
My husband's an *offcomed-un,*
but he likes our Yorkshire brew.
Our down-to-earth, straight-to-the-point
no messing, point of view.
The Brontes learned about it as
they roamed upon the moors,
and wrote their vivid stories
among its crags and tors.
I've travelled t'wide world over,
but there's nowt that can compare
wi' Yorkshire folk and Yorkshire
beer and Yorkshire's good fresh air!

Jean Russell

HEBDEN BRIDGE

The Tourist Trap
Sell antiques and you'll grow fat
Summer weekends - just stay indoors
The tourists have come from over the moors.

Off-comed once have no disguise
It's so apparent that they're *street-wise*
On the pavement, for me, there is no room
For they stand their ground - just like *High Noon.*

Sampling ice creams and fish and chips
Me, shopping to do, but can't get to grips
Who gets the benefit from this trade?
Not locals, like me, I'm afraid.

Roads are choc-a-block each side
We can't escape; or take a bus ride
Long for winter; or a rainy day
When *they* tend to stay away.

But then, when all is said and done
When I go away to have some fun
Then I am *The Tourist* - tables turned,
But the lesson is here to be learned.

Angela Sutcliffe

MY YORKSHIRE

My Yorkshire Moors, so bleak and cold,
With cosy hamlets nestling in its folds,
People's for centuries, hardy and true,
They wouldn't live anywhere else,
They wouldn't know how to.
Sheep farmers, buying and selling their stock,
The well-dressing villages time forgot.
Once seen, the Yorkshire Dales
Haunts everyone's memory,
To return they never fail.
Industry too, plays its part,
Each town centre has its throbbing heart.
The crown of this gem,
York Minster, soaring high,
Rules its domain, o'er all it sees,
Will forever be home to me.

Joan Machen

DESOLATION - SOUTH YORKSHIRE

Bleak towering furnaces
Abandoned like the coal mine shaft
Scene of desolation neath a watering sky
Pipes and bricks and concrete blocks
Wet and slime and rust,
Where once stood men in sweaty rags
In man made hell on earth.

Gone are the heroes of the past
Who fought the breathless heat
With feet in clogs and tongs in hand
On endless summer days
'Side dirty river Don.

The clatter of the bogey wheels
And slitting in the mill
The change of shift and greetings
With clocking off and on.
The noise and hammers thumping
The endless dust and dirt
Are now a distant echo
A murmur on the wind.

Raymond Softley

SURROUNDING HUDDERSFIELD

Around Huddersfield there are the mills
But beauty one can see from many hills
On one hill there is a very old castle
Above fields where graze horses and cattle

Also an old church of years past
Built of stone with seats of pine
And through all the storms and blast
It shows it's stood the test of time

Holmfirth is very fine
Now the *home of summer wine*
Lepton with views so good
Of hills and lovely woods

Honley is also worth a visit
Meltham, Marsden and Scissett
The radio mast on Pole Moor
We didn't have in days of yore

Now it brings entertainment
To every house and tenement
So with castle, church and views
It's better than any city mews.

Joan M Middleton

RAIN OVER THE YORKSHIRE MOORS

Above, a grey as uncompromising as granite,
A hovering, glowering sky told its tale
As unremitting as death itself
It poured out rain as from a culvert.
The birds have all taken flight
Just as the weather's might
Was at its fiercest.
A bleary, blustery wind turns
All the heather into a series
Of small bouquets, still shaken in the storm.
Everywhere around, the only denizens
Of the bleak moors and home to them,
The sheep like great blobs of white paint
Congregate in odd numbers
Telling of hardship in the latter days . . .

Stephen Dyson Taylor

ROBINWOOD

When I was small, I used to walk to school
through fields of flowers.
Pick daisies, and the buttercups
to while away the hours.
Sometimes it made me late for school
the teacher got quite cross.
She stood me in a corner
to show who was boss.
I liked my teacher very much
she used to give me a penny
for getting all my sums correct,
if I failed I wouldn't get any.
I loved my years at Robinwood
and now it's been closed down
but they can't close down my memories,
they'll always be around . . .

Janice Bailey

YORKSHIRE (WE ARE TWO OF A KIND)

Yorkshire, oh Yorkshire,
You were always on my mind,
Yorkshire, oh Yorkshire,
We are two of a kind.

For I've heard it said,
That nothing compares to you
And now, I know, that this much is so true.

And there have been times,
When I thought that I knew best,
But alas, these thoughts, couldn't stand the simplest of tests.

And therefore one day, I know,
That the clouds will roll away
And Yorkshire, oh Yorkshire,
I'll come back to stay.

James Lee

A CELEBRATION OF NORTH YORKSHIRE

The vales, the dales and rambling moors,
North Yorkshire's special beauty,
The blue skies and the fields so green,
Are amongst the best I've ever seen.
North Yorkshire, England's biggest county, is full of friendly faces,
We celebrate the sport of kings, with sunny days at the races.
We've Selby, Harrogate, Northallerton, Thrisk, Scarborough
                                                    and Wetherby,
York, Ripon, Malton and Knaresborough, but to name a few,
Each one has that special charm, something old and new.
All of them with character and many a splendid view.
This county has much history, the land of time lies here.
Across her great green landscapes, many feet have marked this
                                        way, Vikings, Romans, Saxons too,
Down the vistas of time, they've all passed through.
You'll find the warmest welcome here at any time of year,
At our cosy Inns across the county, with the finest hand pulled beer.
The food's good too, with fine home cooking and there's always
                                                         lots to do,
Museums, castles, abbeys and parks with wonderful open spaces,
Towns and villages with plenty to see, there are so many
                                                         lovely places.
Oh, how can I tell you about North Yorkshire, in a poem?
There's just not enough room.
But I'm sure if you visit, you'll see for yourself, and want to come
                                                        back pretty soon.
From the North to the South, from the East to the West,
We're England's biggest county, and for me, one of the best.

Angela McLaughlin

VALENTINE TO SCARBOROUGH

O Scarborough fair, beyond compare,
   My chosen love my life to share,
How often have I sung your praise!
   How often walked through glen and park
In summer shine and winter dark,
   And loved your sea-green ways.

From Cloughton Wyke to Cayton Bay,
   Twice daily crowned in jewelled spray,
O happy rock and shell!
   For they, in golden furrows sown,
In rooted bliss, have centuries known
   The magic of your spell.

What woman born - what charmed unique,
   Could match your Phoenix-like mystique,
Or rouse such mass devotion?
   For yearly at your season's song
One hundred thousand lovers throng
   In fervent adoration.

Like pilgrims treading hallowed ground,
   Wide-eyed your worshippers shuffle round
Processional in every street;
   Near-naked, storm your templed sea,
And day-long bask in ecstasy,
   Kissing your sandalled feet.

O Scarborough fair, beyond compare,
   How hard it is your love to share,
So many hold you dear;
   Yet not for me their fond farewells,
For yearlong sound sweet wedding-bells
   Deep in my resident ear.

Ted Harben

MOORLAND SHEEP

The sheep who shaped this countryside
    Of heather-covered vistas wide,
Of close-cropped turf where red grouse pass
    Through rolling waves of cotton-grass,
Oh, what a debt we owe to them,
For giving us this lovely gem
    Set into Yorkshire's crown.

Their quiet ways become them so,
    They gently graze with heads bent low,
They never deem to cause a riot,
    Or any deed, to spoil our quiet
Enjoyment of their purple land.
We'll never see a sight more grand,
    Than sheep upon the down.

J T Gatenby

PIT FIRE

The siren howls,
I hear it like a hound dog far away.
I wrap my fear within my shawl,
And, shivering, I pray.

'Keep him cold,
Freeze him in the flame,
Rewind him to the start
And play him back to me again.

Let me see him run
Score the winning try,
Bring back the cup, I'll drink the dregs,
But God, don't let him die.'

The cables whine,
The shaft-wheel rattles as it turns,
Death calls, and I stand and frozen as my loved-one burns.

Mary Froggett

THE YORKSHIRE SCENE

A soft, verdant green, with trees between
A vista of sky, purpling by.
A grey, drystone wall, and peace over all,
This is the Yorkshire scene.

There is lowing of cow, over the brow,
And lambs in the fold, a joy to behold.
The beautiful Nidd, and treacherous Strid,
Red sunset on tarn and stream.

There is Scarborough in swing,
And gannet on wing.
Tall ships into Hull, and black-headed gull.
Mysterious legends abound.

Oh, sweet Filey Bay, and Harrogate's Stray.
The old Stamford Bridge, and Garrowby's Ridge.
With York Minster proud, and Bridlington crowd.
Tanned fishermen setting sail.

Bleak moorland, and fell; and small, leafy dell.
Go deep in the dales, hear the old farmers' tales.
Such fair seasons all, from winter to fall,
Here in the Yorkshire scene.

Kathleen Rudd

THE YORKSHIRE SEASONS

Winter wears his mantle white,
Stars reflect in pools of light,
Chill winds 'mid icy chasms chase,
To grip all in their cold embrace.

Winter leads the way to spring,
First flowers to the light to bring,
Snowdrop and daffodil with nodding bloom,
Signal the end to winter's gloom.

Fresh green upon the tree appears,
Bird to growing limb endears,
Standing with roots deep in the land,
Holds nest with strong, but gentle hand.

Summer holds her golden orb on high,
Bright dressed in gown of bluest sky,
From earth, as if on actor's cue,
Spring myriad blossoms of ev'ry hue.

Now the shorter days begin,
And harvest soon is gathered in,
Autumn leaves fall to the ground,
In homage as winter's head is crowned.

Dennis Dunham

WAT

No, am none bain out t'neet, am stopin in bi t' fire.
Ay, a knows wat neet it is, it's neet fur t' flipin choir.
A suppose al a t' tell thee wat 'appened t' other neet
But, al tell thee wat it shames mi, fur a nearly casued a feght.
Ee, now av gone an shocked thi, tha face as gone fair white.
No, dunt tha go un fret thi sen, fur a knows that a were reet.
See, choirmasters getten a cowd, an so 'ee sent 'is sun.
A wish tha could ave erd im Flo, ee knows is stuff bye gum!
T' rehursal went fair splendid, until ee taps 'is stick.
Then, lookin or t'basses, ee ses, 'Now come on Dick,'
'You must sing *what* not *wat*, I'm sure you will agree.'
A ses, wat's wat ave allus sung, an am none bairn change fur thee!
Wi that there were an uproar, an sum said a were reet
But, sum said a were barmy. Ee we'd no more singing that neet.
So, am none bairn out tha sees, am stopin in bit t' fire.
Ee, but al tell thee wat Flo, am fare gon a miss yond choir.

Catherine A Lovett

YORKSHIRE

County of Broad Acres,
Of infinite variety.
Waterfalls and wild rocks,
Hills rolling to the sea,
Deep dales under wide skies,
A land steeped in history;
See the Wolds, a patchwork
Of brown and green and gold
Where many a group of trees
Guards burial mounds of old.
Come with me and stand
Upon the highest hill
And look across the land
To see the sunset glow
Behind the Minster towers;
Warm as the Yorkshire welcome
Given both to friends and strangers.

Winifred V Hipwell

THE YORKSHIRE PUD

Have you heard of Yorkshire pud?
A treat it is indeed.
Especially when you have a lot of hungry kids to feed.

It's all mixed up in the bowl,
And then put in hot tins.
It's cooked in the oven, near the top!
Until it's crispy brown
And when the gravy's poured on top
You've really gone to town!

Now Yorkshire pud, (if it's made just right)
cannot fail to please.
And when the winter winds blow cold
Your tum will *never* freeze.

They eat it in the Yorkshire Dales,
And in the Lowlands too.
It never seems to go amiss whatever
meal you do.

Now all kids brought up on Yorkshire pud
And granny's and grandad's too.
They will always say to you, whatever
comes your way, you really have to
have a Yorkshire pud to make
A perfect day.

Marjorie Langhorn

A MEMORY OF THE DALES

This is my home,
where bloated waters run,
and the weather taunts
the ragged dales.

This is my home,
of sheep and men.
The grey crumbling walls,
weave their ancient way.
This is my home,
where the house on the hill,
could tell,
many
a
tale,
and the trees bow in respect,
of that beautiful land,
that beautiful land.

Caroline Suzanne Collins

THE HAWORTH SPIRIT

Who's ghost, walks the cobbled hill,
When the moon is bright and full?
Who's fading figure, in Victorian garb,
Haunts the bar, of the old Black Bull?
What glowing figures, glide the midnight path,
From the parsonage at Haworth Top
Descending gently, down the cobbled steep,
Floating shop to shop?

Whose glowing figures, stalk the windswept moors,
In the dark and silent night
To the rocky heights, and waterfall,
With ethereal shining light?
Who carries the glowing lantern
In the night, from room to room,
In the parsonage upon the hill,
In the chilling, lowering gloom?

Who's literature, has forever,
This tiny village blessed?
The clinging Haworth, on the hill,
On Mother Pennine's breast.
Will ever such a family,
Grace again this land?
Or does this happen only once,
Through times, slow pouring sand?

Montague M Richards

JUST ANOTHER TOWN

It's just another mining town,
Once a thriving place to live,
Where there's muck there's money
This was true when folk had much to give.

Winding gear dominated the skies,
Heavy lorries transported coal,
A special breed this band of men
Who else would go down the black hole

And what have they done to the market?
Roof of glass, wrought iron sign (Carlton Lanes),
Some say the old was the best
But it's progress, great when it rains.
In time the new will be accepted,
It is built on Roman remains,
A lot of marching's been done before
Time to enjoy the new (Carlton Lanes).

C Whitaker

WET SUNDAY EVENING IN THIRSK

Wide stone square, gracious once,
Cluttered now with waiting cars.
Most shops, all cafés closed,
Only a fish and chip shop sends its tempting smell
Drifting along the street.

Hotels, gold-lettered names brightening the stone,
Promise warmth and comfort, at a price.

Bored adolescents, huddled into anoraks,
Stand aimlessly in twos and threes around wet benches.

Coach travellers, preferring to be home,
Walk disconsolately round the town,
Glancing without interest at shop windows,
Seeking a friendly café offering tea,
Trudging without hope,
For who but a madman would wait for custom
On this wet, bedraggled evening?

Elizabeth Haines

CHAT WITH A PHEASANT

You might think its pleasant
To be a cock pheasant
With feathers all coloured and fine,
But you sure have to run
From the man with the gun
When the beaters are walking in line.

You could say *just fly*
But I can't get too high
I've been eating well all through the year
And to get of the ground
While I'm this fat and round
Is a task I'm not upto my dear.

There's a family I know
Who - when it starts to snow
Put tasty bits outside for me
Which I gobble all up
Like a greedy young pup
Leaving food is bad manners you see.

Now I can't stop to chat
There's a man in a hat
With I rather think evil intent.
So I'll be on my way
Hope you have a nice day.
Then he fluffed up his feathers and went.

Beryl Clayton

BARNOLDSWICK VIA COLNE

Here was a landscape
where no tourist coach would stop;
the picturesque was wanting
merely a mere of millstone grit
set in a rolling sea of green grey hills.
Here were mill chimneys, a family of fourteen
spaced to take advantage of what nature had to offer
behind a sheltering hill
whose springs would water East and West
tributaring Airedale, Ribble and Canal
flowing without prejudice either way.
The townsfolk - county named
had Yorkshire Gills and Cooks from Lancashire
hopscotched in terraces, alternate L and Y.
All weavers, kissed thread end from cops
fed shuttles into warp for cotton cloth.
The clattering looms chattered
rendering down speech to meaningless.
But women weavers gossiping, their lips
told soundless stories of the menfolk
which would prickle hairs
not only on your head.
All must have been Flat Earth Folk
the train stopped here, a single line,
outward was push and coming home was pull - so
miss the train - walk off the edge and fall
into the Unknown Land that's Lancashire.

Albert Thornton

BARLBY IN DECEMBER

Today is the second of the month.
The sky is as white
As the souls of the dead men
That came from the North.
Their wraiths press in
And even the trees look sinister in this light.

Something less than Christian
Has cast its costly, traded silk
Over our bit of Yorkshire.
It is straight from the sadistic heart
Of ice-scorched central Asia.
Sodden, it gets caught on twigs and branches,
Trails in the mud,
And our spirits collapse under it.

The friendly owls have gone.
At night there is silence
And in what passes for day
The crows shout orders to each other
Across torpid, vanquished fields.

I am sinking fast.
The Ouse is rising.
We are counting off the days.

Elizabeth Ryan

MOTHER ROTHER SMOTHER

The smoking chimneys
haze our heritage,
bad shadows that raid our landscape;
the valley's bowel is torn out
and in profusion dumped.
Concrete cooling towers
straddling the tarmac straights
cough out killing fumes,
that hand a dripping spectre
over the woeing hills.
Once where jaunty Hansom cabs,
now tin taxis confuse the green and brown,
of beech and rowan;
black soot splats
belching from the factory taps,
stain the civic sentiment of the town;
industrial sick scape,
capped by rolling mills.
This high iron's hard grip
smothers the rother mother's curves in rust.
Give us back our dying,
unclench your fist on the living,
unleash the wealth that's owing.

Terence David Marshall

WORKING CLASS HEROES

Long, black chimneys bellowing smoke
a sixteen-hour day for t' poor folk
an industrial revolution
or so it were called
more like slave labour
for those involved

They'd wear flat hats
and clogs
live in small, terraced houses
keep pigeons
and dogs
doff their hat to mill owner
and do as their told

Then a great war came
life was never the same
for the few who survived
those who fought for their king
would now fight for their rights
they would never give in

So in t' mill towns
and ridings
the unions grew strong
and laid the foundation
for the true working man.

P G Smith

HOME

Yorkshire, green and brown and gold,
Lonely farms among the folds,
Endless stone walls marching still,
Along the dales and over the hills.
Still higher up, scoured by the weather,
Mile upon mile of purple heather.

Yorkshire changes through the seasons,
Through biting cold winter,
and spring's milder days,
Through summer's vibrant glory,
To autumnal days.
Why leave this county we hold so dear,
With so much beauty to keep us here?

Christine Yeoman

DALES INN TALE

We drove down from deep-snowed north
loud juices squealed for food,
then tucked in beside a hill,
room full of walkers' boots.
Pea soup with toasted garlic bread,
the fire melded us, a taut type said
he trained recruits
for special duties.
'They're up there for a week,'
he indicated ice-veined slopes
and scree above
a tree-filled valley.
'In this weather?'
'They learn to forage
know their strengths and weakness',
and how to cope.
They feed themselves, must not be seen,
points deducted for wood smoke,
scattered rabbit bones.'

He lay back in his fireside chair
and sipped a gin.
Hope they all pass and get a job
like him.

Margaret Foreman

WE'RE ALL BITTER

No lemonade tops,
nor lager louts.
You can tell it's the north
and not the south.

They can keep all their raves,
and their fancy clubs,
I'll stick to the beer
served in Yorkshire's pubs.

They're thought of as grim,
but I have always found,
Yorkshiremen only bitter,
when it's their round.

Deborah Scott

A JOURNEY UP WHARFEDALE

Spectacular views - like the one at Bull Scar,
Better on foot than viewed from a car.
Arriving at Burnsall, cool, clear streams,
Limestone scenery, dramatic ravines.
Skylarks singing, the curlews call,
Rabbits scampering for cover under a wall.
On the horizon is Conistone Pie and
A criss-cross of meadows beneath a lovely, blue sky.
Such a patchwork of landscape,
Whatever the season,
The contentment, the challenge,
Whatever the reason.

Susan Collen-Mawer

ROTHERHAM MEMORIES

Rotherham, Rotherham
Was magic
For me.
I was only three.

Dolls' house,
Dolls,
Santa Claus
And a
Christmas tree,
Market stalls
And baby chicks
Had them
All of course.
I can tick.

I am old with my
Memories.
I can see a house
And me on a chair
Looking for
Presents
They were always there.

At the top
Of a Yorkshire dresser
The wood was gleaming and
Bright.
The blue and white and the brasses
Were Mother's delight.
Now I am on my own.

My pen is never still.
I can remember so
Much sometimes.
Memories can make
You ill,
But then I begin
To smile.
I have been around for a long, long
While!

Anne Crehan

HEBDEN BRIDGE 1994

They hung there on the smooth, cream walls.
Resplendent in their oak stained frames.
Sepia brown, stern, sincere.
These windows into yesteryear.
'Just look at this,' the old lady cries,
as on a tram she rests her eyes,
'It never came as far as this!'
'How do you know?' Her friend shouts out,
and 'Where's Hope Baptist?'
'It isn't here!'
'It must be! It's too large to miss!'
'Well, look at that!'
the old men call,
'I don't remember that stone wall!
and that's young - what's he called again?
Now, wait, his name is in my brain,
We'll never see his like again.'
He were a credit to this town,
all smiling there, in Sepia brown.
His old friend peers across to see
the photographic legacy.
'You daft old fool! Yon lad is me!'

Margaret Walker

YORKSHIRE

This is the place I love to be,
dear old Yorkshire so good to see
with its hills and dales and pastures green
to any place, it's far supreme.

Those ancient castles, ancestral homes,
beauty beyond compare
A little bit of heaven
you won't find anywhere

Princes' have come their brides to find

For Yorkshire they knew
they would find their kind
which would prove to be
a jewel in the crown for all to see.

So here's to good, old Yorkshire
friendly folks and smiling faces
welcomes all
let's sing its praises

Raise the flag
beat the drum
three cheers
for good, old Yorkshire
everyone.

Mary Thompson

LIFE IN SOUTH YORKSHIRE

You have to live in South Yorkshire,
To experience the feelings that are here.
It's hard to believe what has happened to us
And is happening again this year.

Our whole way of life has been taken,
It is not what it used to be.
For proud men and women are broken.
Take a walk through South Yorkshire and see.

Take a long walk through Dinnington or Thurcroft.
Take a good look at the faces you meet.
You could easily mistake them for zombies,
As you pass them by on the street.

It's hard to believe that South Yorkshire's proud men.
Once stood side by side, digging coal,
And then 'twas decided to shut down the pits,
And put the poor souls on the dole.

Take a good walk through Hatfield or Bentley.
See the look of bewilderment there.
For what will their future be now?
Does anyone really care?

South Yorkshire, my friend, is slowly dying.
Once proud, is now fading away.
Its pride and its guts have been taken.
It's so sad to see it this way.

So spare a thought for South Yorkshire,
If ever you're passing through.
And get on your knees, and ask God what you see.
May never happen to you.

Keith Frederick Stringer

A SPECIAL SKILL

When me mother were twelve years old,
She went to work in t'mill.
Half a day as a *tenter*
To learn a special skill.

'Now you larn to be a weaver,'
Is what her mother said.
'Just get it in yer fingers
An' then you will be med.'

So with reed hook, comb and scissors
In t' pocket of her fent,
And shiny clogs a clatterin',
Off to t'mill she went.

She soon picked up that special skill,
Her fingers moved so quick.
She'd to mind t'flying shuttles,
Whirring belts and pickin' sticks.

The mill was damp and noisy,
She couldn't hear folks talk,
An' there were no room 'tween th'alleys
If she went for a walk.

She never med much money,
Even when she had six loom.
Weavers allus were exploited,
Even in the cotton boom.

Now it's a bygone era,
There's no more need for t'mill.
But it's still part of our heritage -
That very special skill.

Edna Beach

HALFWAY HOUSE TWIXT NORTH AND SOUTH

My husband was born in Newcastle
But found his new wife in the South;
One daughter was born in Glamorgan
The other was born in Tynemouth.

Halfway twixt the two, in South Yorkshire,
A county we've come to love dear;
For almost a quarter of a century,
We've brought up our family here.

We thought that when we retired,
We might move back south or p'raps north,
But our girls have put down their roots here
So we're going to stay here henceforth.

Historical places abound here:
Roche Abbey's a gem in its vale
And Conisbrough Castle is well worth a visit,
As Walter Scott wrote in his tale.

There are so many stretches of water
To which birdwatchers like me travel far,
To Denaby Ings and Sprotbrough Flash,
Wath Ings and Potteric Carr.

There's no shortage if you are a shopper,
Sheffield is a marvellous place
Especially now Meadowhall's there,
But Doncaster is more to my taste.

My husband and I dearly love walking
And many a mile do we roam;
But it's wonderful at the end of the day
To return to our South Yorkshire home.

Cynthia Cooksley

WILLOWHERB

In August as the summer fades
and leaves take on a darker green
the rosebay willowherb invades
and decorates the scene.

It commandeers unwanted ground
in tall formations closely set,
and every stem will soon be crowned
with its own coronet.

The pink and purple clusters spread
a mantle over nature's scars -
the rubbish dump, the ruined shed
and the abandoned cars.

Some call it *fireweed,* for it grows
on bomb site or volcanic ash
and in unlikely places shows
its colourful panache.

Beneath an ever-changing sky,
where flowers were never seen before,
its purple patches beautify
the weather-beaten moor.

It marks a season of the year
with its own character and name,
then withers in the colder air
and fades as quickly as it came.

John Browne